Believing in South Central

Believing in
South Central

EVERYDAY ISLAM
IN THE CITY OF ANGELS

Pamela J. Prickett

The University of Chicago Press CHICAGO AND LONDON

The University of Chicago Press, Chicago 60637
The University of Chicago Press, Ltd., London
© 2021 by The University of Chicago
Published 2021
Printed in the United States of America

30 29 28 27 26 25 24 23 22 21   1 2 3 4 5

ISBN-13: 978-0-226-74714-9 (cloth)
ISBN-13: 978-0-226-74728-6 (paper)
ISBN-13: 978-0-226-74731-6 (e-book)
DOI: https://doi.org/10.7208/chicago/9780226747316.001.0001

Library of Congress Cataloging-in-Publication Data

Names: Prickett, Pamela J., author.
Title: Believing in South Central : everyday Islam
in the City of Angels / Pamela J. Prickett.
Other titles: Everyday Islam in the City of Angels
Description: Chicago ; London : The University of Chicago
Press, 2021. | Includes bibliographical references and index.
Identifiers: LCCN 2020037870 | ISBN 9780226747149 (cloth) |
ISBN 9780226747286 (paperback) | ISBN 9780226747316 (ebook)
Subjects: LCSH: African American Muslims—California—Los
Angeles. | African American Muslims—California—Los Angeles—
Social conditions. | African Americans—California—Los Angeles—
Social conditions. | Los Angeles (Calif.)—Social conditions.
Classification: LCC F869.L89 N365 2020 | DDC 305.896/073079494—dc23
LC record available at https://lccn.loc.gov/2020037870

♾ This paper meets the requirements of ANSI/NISO Z39.48-1992
(Permanence of Paper).

In loving memory

L.E.P.
who first believed in me
R.M.H.
who taught me to believe again

Allah is the Protector of those who have faith
from the depths of darkness
He will lead them forth into light.
AL BAQARAH 2:257

Contents

Living a Muslim Way of Life
in South Central

Sister Ava loved watching movies. She kept a portable television with built-in DVD player in the back of her rusted baby-blue Dodge van, just in case she wanted to have a movie night at the *masjid* (mosque) or in her front yard. Her DVD collection, which she kept locked in her room, was extensive—no streaming video for this sixty-seven-year-old lifelong resident of Los Angeles. She didn't trust the internet for anything except ordering material goods, the kind you could resell. When it was time for a movie night, she pulled two or three DVDs at a time. Mostly, these were fun, fluffy films offering a welcome distraction from the stress of everyday life. Romantic comedies starring American sweethearts, action-packed blockbusters featuring pirates and superheroes, and quirky British comedies were among her favorites. Sometimes, though, the movies had deeper plots, and Ava's film analyses became critical ruminations on life and love. Every so often, she insisted I watch these special films as part of her teaching.

That was the case one night in 2014. We sat inside the van, which was parked on her lawn—the same lawn where she sometimes set up folding tables to feed the neighborhood's homeless people after Ramadan. From the TV, propped between the front bucket seats, we ran an extension cord to the side of the yellow Victorian that was home to Ava and three of her siblings. Next, Ava put *Life of Pi* into the DVD player and we settled back, tucked under thick blankets, to watch the two-hour film about Pi, a sixteen-year-old Indian boy who survives a shipwreck by escaping in a lifeboat with a Bengal tiger. Based on a book with the same title, the Oscar-winning film promises a story that will make you believe in God. As the story unfolds, the movie becomes a cinematic meditation on how we wrestle metaphorical tigers in our human quest for meaning and faith. One reviewer wrote, "This story is a Gedankenexperiment for the worst-case scenario, a modern-day story of Job, all about how you can find spirituality and the meaning of life in the throes of all that is horrible and terrible in the world today."[1] As the film moves through Pi's journey across the sea, a moral emerges: in life's moments of savagery and pain, you can choose to see God as having abandoned you or, as Pi does, you can choose to believe that God is present at every moment. Spoiler alert: because Pi keeps faith, the tiger becomes his savior, protecting the boat as they float to eventual safety.

For weeks, Ava built up *Life of Pi* to me, urging me to find time to come over and watch. The movie prompted her to ask me (and herself) hard questions: Do you see Allah through your worst struggles? Are you praying for what *you* want or for what *Allah wants for you*? According to Ava, it better be the latter if you are a true believer, and your faith must never waiver, no matter the degree of struggle. Of course, the sociologist in me knows that some of us will wrestle more often and with bigger beasts, for life is an unequal journey across the sea. After nearly seven decades of living as a Black woman in South Central LA, Ava knew it too. But even if life doesn't go as you intend, Ava believed that it's in the striving that we find self-worth and our own agentic potential.

Ava's faith was indeed unwavering despite the storms that rocked her. In the past decade, she had faced repeated difficulty in paying her bills, health problems, threats of violence directed at her children and grandchildren, and a seemingly never-ending set of family quarrels. She chose to see Allah as present through all of it, constructing Islam into a moral force to propel her through life. And it was this deep belief coursing through her veins that kept her participating in Masjid al-Quran, the mosque down the street where we had met seven years earlier, even when its leaders and other believers drove her mad with their backstabbing and alleged corruption. She brought tears to my eyes that night as she recounted her commitment to Islam, reaffirmed in watching the movie.

*   *   *

Believers in this long-standing religious community see Islam as a *way of life* in South Central that offers a blueprint for individual and collective action promising greater social, economic, and political progress. Imam Mustafa Khalid, head religious authority at Masjid al-Quran (or MAQ, as I call it in this book) and its leader for more than forty years, said, "Our religion is a comprehensive religion . . . [not] simply *a* religion. That's why it's called a way of life. The perfect way of life Allah has designed." This, according to Khalid, means the "Islamic message follows us wherever we go, as we go about business in society, socialize with our friends, and in our relationships." The Arabic term for this faith or way of life is *din* (pronounced *deen* at MAQ), and it represents "a correlation between orthodoxy—*right ideas*, or faith—and orthopraxis—*right actions*."[2] This relationship between belief and action is best thought of as one similar to theory and activism: "One is internal and the other is external. One is hidden and the other is manifest—and at best, a manifestation of the internal."[3] In their actions with and toward one another, believers at MAQ express their personal faith.

In this book, I examine how MAQ members come together to live a contemporary Muslim way of life. To do so requires a broader conception of piety, one that examines expected rituals (i.e., prayer, veiling) but also social, political, and economic practices that believers engage in together with the intent of deepening their faith. To explain, I expand on the work of late anthropologist Saba Mahmood, who researched the women's mosque movement in Egypt.[4] But where Mahmood explored how Islam fosters individual subject formation, I am interested in how believers of this faith construct a moral community. Mahmood showed that it was through "forms of submission internal to different constructions of freedom"— namely, embodied religious practices—that participants further their own ends of cultivating a more ethical self.[5] For example, women in her study practiced veiling (wearing a head scarf) as a means of modesty, which they saw as a virtue of Islamic piety. This meant that veiling was a conscious act that served as both a *critical marker* and the *ineluctable means* by which the women trained themselves to be pious.[6] "One cannot simply discard the veil once a modest deportment has been acquired," Mahmood argued, "because the veil itself is part of what defines that deportment."[7] In this way, agency is understood as a person's ability to act that may, at times, involve willing subordination. This seems counterintuitive to many Western conceptions of agency, thought to be the expression or realization of free will. However, according to Mahmood, within Islam a person may choose to submit to something restrictive in pursuit of something deeper. Therefore, Mahmood describes women in the mosque movement as "virtuosos of piety," their embodied actions like those of a pianist who willingly calluses the hands in pursuit of art.[8]

Piety at MAQ involves the cultivation of virtues that must be achieved through engagement with others. As Imam Khalid said, "Islam doesn't believe in isolation. *Our test is living a community life*." Taking this back to Mahmood's work, veiling for the women in her study was not merely a way to signify a religious identity but a way to *shape* the religious self. Similarly, in this study, living a community life is not only a way to express a religious identity but also a constitutive component of one's din. It requires a form of religious consciousness, called *taqwa*, that is supposed to teach the indi-

vidual self-restraint, virtue, and right conduct. This is not piety indepen-
dent of others, as typical measures of religiosity capture. Emanating "from
within the person out into the realm of actions," *taqwa* may be best thought
of as a form of moral consciousness that organizes social life.[9] Community
becomes as much a part of one's piety as individual acts such as prayer.
Even prayer must at times be communal, with the notion of congregation
woven into worship services on Islam's holiest day of the week. Friday's *jumah salat* (congregational prayer) takes place inside the prayer hall (*musal-
lah*) and includes a brief *khutbah* (sermon) followed by a special organized
prayer that aims to bring Muslims together, their feet side-by-side to create
a united prayer line. This is just one of the ways in which believers interpret
Islam as providing "rules and regulations" for how to live with one another.
As a visiting imam said during one of his Friday khutbahs, "[Islam] is a way
of life that establishes the individual. The individual. If I can live this way of
life as an individual, and you can live this way of life as an individual, when
we combine these individualities together we're forming a righteous community." A righteous community is the goal, and it follows in all that the
women and men in this book do in the course of their daily lives.

In the pages that follow, I examine how members of MAQ draw from
the mosque community for social support in a changing urban landscape,
the ways the local environment shapes the forms of this support, and the
gender and class dimensions of organized religious support. As they seek to
provide care to one another while engaging faith, believers encounter social
problems that pull their resources and attention from intended aims, including a lack of resources, competition, broken relationships, and threats
of violence. The book's key strength is in showing how and why believers work through interpersonal and communitywide conflicts in order to
deepen their engagement with Islam and their commitment to South Central. These collective actions enable members to further a project of religious self-making that bonds African American Muslim women and men
together. They cannot discard community any more than the women in
Mahmood's study could not discard the veil.

* * *

Living a Muslim way of life and seeking to follow Islam in all one does are
incumbent on all Muslims, but that doesn't mean that all Muslims engage
faith on a level playing field. For those living in a Muslim-majority society,
it may be easier to follow certain practices, such as fasting (*sawm*) during Ramadan, because the entire society slows down. Believers at MAQ
liked to point out that in places like Saudi Arabia, much of daily business

is suspended, while believers in the United States must keep up with work and home matters at the same pace as the non-Muslim majority. There are challenges outside Ramadan too. Believers may find it difficult to get time off work on Fridays to attend jumah, which begins promptly at MAQ at 1:00 p.m. And they may struggle with keeping their finances in accordance with *shari'ah* (Qur'anic law), as there are fewer *halal* (permissible) banking and credit services available in the West.

There also will be uneven challenges *within* non-Muslim societies, as in the United States. The Muslim American community may be the most diverse in the world, but it is also one of the most divided by race and class. Arab and South Asian Muslims outrank African American Muslims on measures of occupational status and educational attainment.[10] When racial and class differences within a religious category align with structural inequalities in US society, it may reinforce and even perpetuate disadvantage.[11] The interlocking systems of inequality within American religion help explain why religious organizations are among the most segregated spaces in our society.[12]

MAQ members had abundant experience in working through struggles, because engaging Islam had long been a complex matter in this community. They expressed a deep pride in their five decades in South Central, but at times this history cast a dark shadow over the community itself, obscuring its ability to see the challenges it faced. Under the Nation of Islam, MAQ established brick and mortar businesses in the neighborhood in the 1960s and early 1970s, including restaurants, grocery stores, and bakeries as well as an international fish import business and a prominent newspaper sold throughout the South Central region. Further raising the community's profile on local streets were the designated Fruit of Islam (FOI) "soldiers" who patrolled the neighborhood to promote social order and monitor activities. Said Imam Khalid of this time, "We lived in the neighborhood, and for the most part we prevented violence." Through its efforts, the MAQ community could recruit members steadily through the first two decades of its history.

Then in a series of financial setbacks in the mid-1970s, the community lost most of its brick and mortar businesses. Items once sold in retail shops, like clothing and food, were now being sold out of cars and plastic crates on the mosque grounds. The lack of personal and community financial resources made believers feel pinched after previous years of plenty. Compounding the community's economic downturn was the loss of jobs in South Central as factories left the area and the local economy shifted to the service sector. Poverty rates rose and continued to do so throughout the 1990s. Then came the waves of drug- and gang-related violence that made South Central infamous during the 1980s.[13] Around the same time, the neighborhood underwent a dramatic demographic shift from majority Black to Latino, caused by an influx of new migrants from Central America coupled with the outmigration of thousands of African Americans. The latter began moving to better neighborhoods in the 1970s, but in the 1980s their exodus accelerated as gangs drove out many families. Gone were the future recruits receptive to the idea of Islam as a tool of urban-racial transformation, the religious ecology now favoring the faiths of new residents, such as Catholicism and Pentecostalism. By the early 1990s, the once great former Nation of Islam temple that believers had purchased in cash was gone—literally demolished. The city had declared the building unsafe, and the MAQ community was too short on funds to rebuild—hence its makeshift properties still in place in 2008 when I started my fieldwork. Leaders have been hustling ever since to raise funds to rebuild, their attempts repeatedly thwarted by suspicions of corruption, a dwindling membership base, and a tightening of donations from overseas after 9/11.

As the MAQ community's history became defined more by loss than by growth, the intensity with which believers turned to Islam as a framework for social change increased. Members fellowshipped with other Muslim communities, sometimes across ethnic lines, but more often they amped up their internal efforts. The need to make money became particularly strong for them after decades of high unemployment in South Central. However, in accordance with their efforts to live a Muslim way of life, moneymaking had to be conducted in compliance with Islamic guidelines for moral action. That was why the mosque transformed into a marketplace, which became an organizing force for building community. Believers relied on one another to meet their material needs through the buying and selling of *halal* goods, with participation intended to redefine financial loss as a calling to a stronger work ethic. Leaders taught that running a business made believers better Muslims. But, as everyone within the community saw, demand far exceeded supply, and resources weren't sufficient to satisfy members' needs.

*   *   *

Like many members of the mosque, Sister Ava had been living in a state of economic insecurity for decades if not most of her life. She survived on a fixed income of $835 per month, earning just over $10,000 in reported annual income—this in a city where celebrities frequently flaunt spending as much on a handbag via their social media posts. There's no such luxury in Ava's LA, just twelves miles yet a world away from the 20th Century Fox

Studios that produced *Life of Pi*. Once divorced and once widowed, she has spent most of her adult life working two or more jobs at the same time in order to feed and clothe her kids. As a single mom, it wasn't always possible for her to give them the attention they needed, and she confessed on more than one occasion, and through a flood of tears, that she was harsher with her hand than she should have been. Still, Ava insisted that those hardships didn't erase her children's agency. All four of her sons had served time in prison, and she refused to accept that they had no other choices than to sell drugs or engage in the "fast life." She pointed to her own work ethic and frugal living as evidence that someone can survive in South Central without abandoning faith or morality. Like other believers at the masjid, Ava drew a distinct boundary between her off-the-books catering and the illicit activities she saw around her. When one of her sons turned his life around and became a successful entertainer, she bragged not about his higher income but about the shift in his moral code.

Most African American Muslims are converts to the faith, having come to Islam from Christianity. They navigate two religious worlds across two different kinship structures — that of their chosen Muslim family and that of their (often Christian) biological kin.[14] They can't take as a given that their loved ones will understand their religious beliefs and practices the way that Muslims born into a family legacy of Islam can. Members of MAQ must explain to Christian family members why certain cultural practices common among African American communities, like eating pork or drinking alcohol, aren't Islamically permissible. And that's just the tip of the iceberg. One of Ava's blood sisters called the religion "His-lam," expressing outright hostility at how she thought women were treated at the mosque. Even some of Ava's children expressed misgivings about their mom's being Muslim. They held a negative association between Islam and gender because of their late stepfather, whom they perceived as using the religion to exert control over Ava. None of this turned Ava off from Islam or stopped her from attending MAQ, though. In comparing herself to her siblings, she said many times over the years, "I thank Allah every day I'm Muslim!"

Much of the struggle of daily life in the MAQ community involved trying to push past inequality as a community devoted to Islam. This shared moral project took on added meaning because, as a community with relatively little in material resources, doing what was perceived as "right" was sometimes the only way to be respected within MAQ. Other measures of success, such as occupational status, educational attainment, and the accumulation of wealth, were out of reach for most of the mosque participants I studied. They worked but didn't earn enough to meet their needs, often relying on other forms of public and private assistance. Even relatively better-off members struggled to feel as financially secure as they wanted, professing in both front-stage and backstage conversations that they were "poor" or "broke." Yet nearly everyone I met over my years of hanging out in the community thought that identifying as a Muslim made them better off than others in the neighborhood and the non-Muslims in their families. In this way, striving through Islam didn't always lead to measurable material change, though it did feed an intangible yet fundamental need for hope. MAQ members creatively worked their immediate environment and its structural dimensions of urban disadvantage into their formulations of what it means to be Muslim, intending to do right by Allah not in spite of the neighborhood but in direct engagement with it. Participation at the mosque even when it created burdens—indeed *because* it created burdens—helped deepen one's piety. This suggests that religion is complex, not only when different forms of inequality intersect, but when these intersections create a different way of understanding what religion means for people of faith.[15]

Faith and Black Placemaking

From the street, Masjid al-Quran didn't look like much. Surrounded by a wire fence, it was recognizable as a place of worship only if you knew the signs: outdoor shoe racks, sinks for washing hands and feet, and a framed artist's rendering of a future building featuring a dome and minaret. For outsiders, the masjid looked more like a family compound, with its two mismatched houses awkwardly joined by a sinking green awning. The larger house was the prayer hall, a single-story stucco structure with two sliding glass doors for entrances: one for brothers (men) and one for sisters (women). The other house, a small cottage, contained staff offices, a kitchen, the brothers' bathroom with shower, the sisters' powder room, and the bedroom of an elderly brother who had lived on site for as long as anyone could remember. Asked why Brother Kareem stayed there, Sister Ava answered simply, "We were his only family." He used the brothers' bathroom and community kitchen as his own. Most other brothers performed *wudu* (ritual cleansing before prayer) at an outdoor sink near a second men's entrance on the side of the building. For the first three years of the study, sisters used a small powder room inside the house for *wudu*, but they later helped finance the installation of a portable shed next to the house that contained a sink and foot-washing station. All the materials used to piece together the compound were either donated or bought on the cheap, often in different colors and in varying states of wear.

MAQ's physical appearance belied its importance in its members' lives.

The masjid was a place where believers gathered before, during, and long after worship services, often staying late into the night. Brothers played dominoes under a portable tent many afternoons, and sisters used the masjid as a meeting place for social get-togethers as well as a safe space for their children and grandchildren to play. Protected day and night by a team of security guards, the mosque was a safe spot to spend time in a neighborhood considered one of the most dangerous in the city. And even if the property didn't look like much, it was more than others in the neighborhood had. The security team, composed of Brother Elijah and two other men, deflected would-be burglars and kicked out occasional squatters.

Most important, the mosque was where believers made friends for life, as was the case for Sister Ava and her best friend of thirty years, Sister Aisha. Though the women already knew each other through people in the neighborhood, it wasn't until Ava found Islam and started attending MAQ that they hit it off. Their friendship became legendary within the community, with the sixty-something duo spending more time together than Aisha did with her husband. The pair spent many of their days going on what Ava called their neighborhood "adventures," scouting for deals at different stores and visiting friends and family. MAQ served as their hub, their home away from home. And though the women had both watched with sadness as their once great Muslim community in South Central had slowly dwindled to its current state, they could reflect on their decades of friendship as a defining feature of their lives. Sitting next to her best friend at lunch one afternoon, Sister Aisha said, "Our kids grew up together. *That's* community."

Despite national trends suggesting the waning influence of religion in everyday American life, we know that African Americans remain one of the most religious populations in the United States if not *the* most religious. Surveys indicate that African Americans believe in God, pray daily, and say that religion is important to them at rates higher than those for whites and Latinos.[16] Yet we rarely read about the influence of religion on Black urban residents or about how their religion serves as a source of identity that intersects with other markers of social life in their communities. With the exception of a few notable classics in urban ethnography, many scholars give little more than a nod to the churches and mosques that so many African Americans have participated in since the Great Migration.[17] This gap in information is more consequential than just a "scholarly lacuna," because it contributes to a larger tendency in American public life: when talking about Black urban communities, discourse focuses almost exclusively on social problems.[18] As Marcus Hunter and colleagues explain, "Yes, many black people live within a fundamentally racialized and racist structuring of (urban) space and some black people exhibit bad behaviors as a result, but this reality does not wholly consume the energies of the black community. What remains are the creative practices of black placemaking."[19] Such placemaking, as they define it, "refers to the ability of residents to shift otherwise oppressive geographies of a city to provide sites of play, pleasure, celebration, and politics."[20]

In the pages that follow, I give close attention to how identifying as African American *and* Muslim summons a distinct kind of religious identity while situating this summoning in the particular urban place in which it occurs.[21] Of the twenty neighborhoods in Los Angeles with the lowest median incomes, at the time of writing more than half are located in South Central. Sadly, and as some believers know well through personal experience, the twenty deadliest neighborhoods in LA are all part of South Central. The region's urban form gives rise to specific interpretations and enactments of Islam among believers that incorporate this lived reality into constructions of community. In other words, I can't ignore the real and perceived social problems in this setting, but neither can I ignore the laughter and joking woven into how believers made sense of their shared struggles. It is in people's hopes and dreams that we learn what they understand to be their structural realities.

By telling a different kind of story about a Black urban life—one that starts with believers' efforts to build their religious community as the focal point of their lives rather than as a consequence of social problems—this book gives attention to the collective struggles of African Americans striving to conduct themselves in what they see as the Islamic way within a context of financial and moral uncertainty. My observations and analyses focus on the issues that believers focused on: making a living, balancing work and family, cultivating meaningful relationships, and understanding their role in the larger society. These were the main rhythms of life inside the MAQ community. Yes, there were threats of violence from gangs and police, but they appear in this book only insofar as they were part of how the community was organized, how believers differentiated themselves from outsiders, and how they shrugged off some of the issues that other ethnographers have foregrounded. In fact, without ignoring urban struggles, my book can be viewed as an account that helps counter the often bleak portrayals of contemporary African American life in more crime-oriented neighborhood studies. Following the work of Marcus Hunter, Mary Pattillo, and others, I show how belonging, morality, and friendship flourish among believers who identify as urban Black Americans and, importantly, why believers push forward with these efforts as their struggles continue and sometimes intensify.

Within this African American Muslim community, then, Islam offers a practical set of guidelines for living a moral life with the end goal of becoming a better, more righteous community. To understand these guidelines requires that we develop a different way of thinking about piety, one that goes beyond the individual to how people engage faith together. It requires seeing the relationships that members cultivate as part and parcel of how people "do religion."[22] In this way, religion becomes understood as cultural work that people make, moving between religious institutions, texts, rituals, and practices.[23] Emphasis at MAQ is on making religion work within the confines of local structural disadvantages. Believers turn Islam into their tool kit for addressing poverty, racial inequality, and violence. Even more, as a cornerstone of their faith they work together to try to alleviate the problems associated with life in South Central. As I argue throughout this book, in working together as a community, as a religious family, members of the mosque strive to deepen their piety and, in turn, their relationship with Allah.

About the Research

To show how religious belief is a path toward a higher moral project, this book takes readers inside the lives of MAQ's members, who struggle to make ends meet as they simultaneously strive to improve their conditions. From May 2008 to August 2013, I immersed myself in the MAQ community. I participated in and observed a variety of religious and social activities, including jumah, Islamic classes, fund-raising banquets, religious conferences, festivals, and funerals. I volunteered on several planning committees and logged hundreds of hours cooking and cleaning alongside women believers. For thirteen months of the study (2009–10), I lived four blocks from the mosque to better understand the daily realities of life in a neighborhood with concentrated poverty. During my residence in the neighborhood, I spent two to five nights per week at MAQ hanging out with a group of long-standing community members, increasing my visits to nearly every night during the holy month of Ramadan. I also volunteered at a center for at-risk youth, tutoring students from nearby public and charter schools.

In addition to these more than five years of in-depth fieldwork, I continued to gather data in the community for several more years although without the same level of intensity. From August 2013 until May 2015, I made regular visits to MAQ; however, by this time my relationships with members like Ava and Aisha involved spending more time together outside the mosque than in it. I incorporate some of this data into my analyses, but the bulk of my findings derive from the first intense period of fieldwork at MAQ. When I moved out of state in June 2015, my visits over the next four years dropped to three times per year, including at least once per Ramadan. That said, I have maintained close ties to a few members and continue to see them outside the mosque on my return trips to LA. This means that altogether I have spent the better part of ten years studying the MAQ community and benefiting from its wisdom and humor.

The length and breadth of my fieldwork have enabled me to observe interactions among believers at MAQ, between believers and non-Muslim neighbors, and between believers at MAQ and those of other Muslim communities who visited that mosque to give charity. Rare is the mosque in the United States that devotes itself only to prayer, as compared with mosque communities in Muslim-majority countries.[24] In the American context, mosques also provide social and legal services and organize regular community events. These functions develop in part because believers have more opportunities to "shop" different mosques, but mainly because mosques in the United States are voluntary and therefore privately funded.[25] In Saudi Arabia, for example, the government funds local masjids and salaries for imams.

In studying the perspective of a community whose members identify as both Muslim and African American, it may help the reader to know more about the researcher. I came into the project with an explicit intellectual desire to understand the everyday lives of African American Muslims, who have a long, rich history of practicing Islam in the United States yet remain curiously absent from most public and scholarly discussions about the religion. I am a sociologist and an ethnographer who is fascinated by religion, though not a religious person myself. I envy people who take a leap of faith, an envy that grew as I watched the women and men described in this book face extreme hardships and come out the other side deeper in their religious convictions. Believers at MAQ radiate such joy from their commitment to Islam that Arabic words about God's greatness are sometimes the last words they utter in this life. I admire the belief I witnessed and have sought throughout this text not to let hardship overshadow the importance of faith. I am deeply grateful that the women and men in this study have allowed me to be part of their lives, graciously serving as my teachers on many matters of life.[26]

In setting out to study how people at MAQ live Islam, I purposely focused on observing what believers did together, why they chose these actions and not others, and with what consequences. As such, I am able to show how believers draw from faith in the realm of the everyday, including how they dress, what they eat, and how they deal with birth, death, sexuality, and so on.[27] Lived religion can also involve artistic expressions and community traditions meant to create solidarity. Some of these include rituals we easily recognize as religious (e.g., prayer and worship), but research on lived religion also includes activities that may not be obviously or immediately religious to outsiders—activities that cross social, political, economic, and cultural realms. In short, if actions are treated as religious by the people that enact them, that's enough for me to designate these as religious.[28] For example, if believers evoke the sacred in their arguments over how to respond to an inebriated man wanting to get food, as they do in chapter 1, then we must respect this as their way of living Islam. It's not my role as ethnographer to adjudicate what religion is or is not. Rather, it's to show how believers understand their actions in relation to the larger moral project of living their din in this particular urban setting—one marked by decades of disadvantage and structural neglect.

∗   ∗   ∗

Believers at MAQ may see Islam as the solution, but the researcher in me can't ignore that identifying with a stigmatized religion has added to their struggles. They must work out a way of living Islam in an urban space that's not always open to a message of inclusion and at times may be downright hostile toward believers' faith. Many Americans, including most Christians, know little about Islam outside what they read in the news or hear in public discourses, in part because they don't know actual Muslims.[29] Only 45 percent of Americans say they know a Muslim, compared with 86 percent who report they know a Catholic.[30] Without interpersonal contact, it becomes easier to Other Muslims. This partly explains why Americans hold a more negative view of this religious population than any other in the United States, including atheists.[31] In other words, identifying with Islam may create new struggles for believers at MAQ, even if it wasn't something they often discussed. All Muslims in the United States face stigma, but how it's experienced differs by race, class, gender, and neighborhood.[32]

Estimates suggest there are more than 1 million African American Muslims, with as many as one-fourth attending mosques in inner-city neighborhoods.[33] The code for those women and men is one built around the Qur'an, not "the street."[34] Often mistaken as "Black Muslims" in the Nation of Islam, members of MAQ actually share more theologically with the millions of practicing Muslims in Indonesia than with the current and highly controversial leader of the Nation of Islam, Louis Farrakhan. In fact, let me make clear: this is *not* a book about "Black Muslims." The term is a misnomer, coined by a sociologist in the 1960s to refer to the members of the

Nation of Islam. As Imam Khalid said in a public lecture one year, "C. Eric Lincoln gave us that name through the book *Black Muslims in America*. [It] was not a name of our choosing." Nor was it one that members used except to mock the ways outsiders viewed them and misunderstood what the Nation did as a movement.[35]

Among this community of African American Muslims in South Central, Islam was once a buffer against racial and class marginalization, but with the decline of the Nation of Islam and growing intolerance toward Islam in the post-9/11 United States, their faith also becomes a liability at times. This book describes what it means for African Americans to live a Muslim way of life in a neighborhood of changing demographics and disadvantages. It examines how African American Muslims draw from their religious tradition to navigate local life, even if it causes more complications. Having visited other *masajid*, I know there are particularities to how Islam is engaged at MAQ, but it's the specific ways that believers in this study work out a way of being Muslim that enable fresh perspectives on Islam.

Sometimes, it seemed as though competition and distrust would overwhelm the MAQ community, especially because few new members or resources were entering the circuits of exchange at the mosque. On the other hand, as believers expressed many times during my fieldwork, they had survived far worse over their decades of living and worshipping in South Central—threats that included urban riots, police intimidation, decreasing jobs, and the spillover effects of gang and drug violence. They took tremendous pride in the fact that their tattered mosque had stayed planted in the same disadvantaged neighborhood for more than fifty years, and seeing themselves as kin made members more willing to stick it out. Ava said, "We're like a family down here. . . . We fight like family, but [we're] still family."

CHAPTER ONE

"Our Test Is Living
a Community Life"

Sister Ava rushes around the kitchen, moving between several stainless-steel catering pans on the counter. The silver pans are filled with *halal* baked chicken, rice, roasted vegetables, beans, and salad. Sister Aisha is stirring a large pot of lamb stew on the stove. Without prompting, she moves her body so Ava can open the oven door and grab another dish. Meanwhile, Sister Dina sits at the kitchen table slicing strawberries to go atop a cream-cheese cake that Ava had baked this morning. I ask Aisha whether she went to jumah today, and she tells me yes but adds nothing more. Tension is palpable, with the women less talkative than usual. In less than twenty minutes, the Masjid al-Quran lot will fill with fasting believers ready for *iftar*, their first meal in over fourteen hours, and the food is not done.

Normally, Ava would cook at her home ten blocks away, where its commercial-grade stove allows her to work faster. But after "drama" with one of her siblings there, she escaped to the masjid and called on her Muslim sisters to help make the sunset deadline. Ava asks me to walk with her to get more supplies from her van. Stepping out of the kitchen and holding her arms close to her body, she jiggles her right hand downward at the side of her upper thigh, saying she needs "to shake the *jin* [evil spirit] away." She feels that her din was being tested by the turmoil at home, the evil threatening to ruin both her ability to feed the community and the overall spirit of her Ramadan. She would have missed the sunset deadline had she not been able to rely on her Muslim sisters to help her—women Ava called her angels sent by Allah. Together, the women could get enough food ready for iftar to begin on time and for the community to earn its blessings for feeding the poor that night.

During the sacred month of Ramadan, believers abstain from food, drink, and sexual activity during sunlight hours. Those who accept this commitment will go so much as eighteen hours without even a sip of water—a feat made more daunting by Southern California's dry summer heat. Yet believers at MAQ rarely complained about fasting. More often, they said they welcome the experience as a way to deepen their din, demonstrate gratitude for Allah's revealing the Qur'an, and practice self-discipline.[1] In a study of recent converts to Islam, fasting (*sawm*) was regarded as one of several possible forms of religious abstinence that helped pious newcomers form a morally constitutive self.[2] It "produces a powerful change in the body that serves to disrupt one's ability to engage with and make sense of the social world in taken-for-granted ways."[3]

For many observers outside Islam, including Western academics and journalists, the embodied effects of the lack of food and drink seem to be the most challenging part of Ramadan. Every year, major US newspapers profile fasting Muslim Americans, focusing on how they manage work and school. Often, these papers devote special attention to athletes who fast amid the extreme physical exertion of professional sports.[4] But as important as what believers *refrain from* during Ramadan is what they *engage in* for those thirty days and nights—performing greater acts of charity and striving to improve their social behaviors. *Zakat*, technically a tax on one's wealth but interpreted at MAQ more loosely as charity, is one of the five pillars of Islam. The hunger and thirst that fasting brings to the body teach observers to show compassion for people who face hunger regularly. "It challenges you as a human," one member told me. "If you think you better than the poor, your belly's hungry too." In other words, believers make the act of self-sacrifice a deeply conscious social practice meant to raise awareness about relative privilege. Every year, Imam Khalid, head religious authority at MAQ, reminded believers of these social meanings of the fasting month. "Ramadan is the month the Qur'an was revealed," he said. "It is the month of patience, the month of sympathy. We sympathize with the less fortunate of the immediate community and in the world."

More than any other time of the year, believers make a conscious effort during Ramadan to reach out to those they perceive as less fortunate, inviting hungry Muslims and non-Muslims from the neighborhood to come inside the gates of MAQ for a free plate to either eat there or take with them. The meal that Ava and the other sisters cooked together, which believers call iftar, will feed not only fasting believers but also people from the neighborhood living in nearby houses or on the streets. The dinners are designed to help members of the mosque "get blessings" by fulfilling their duty to feed the poor during Islam's holiest month, and they fit within a larger religious mandate the community imposes on itself during Ramadan to increase the frequency and intensity of worship and outreach. The more people who show up at the masjid to eat, the more blessings that Ava and the sponsor who paid her to cook will receive. How believers understand what it means to fulfill a religious obligation to help others is profoundly shaped by their own everyday struggles—namely, constrained resources, overburdened networks, and the threat of neighborhood violence. Consequently, the increased intensity and frequency of worship during Ramadan could compound existing tensions or create new ones. In leaning on religious kin to earn blessings together amid their daily troubles, believers simultaneously deepen their sense of religious selfhood and their bonds with one another.

Though Ava received money for her labor—around $40, on top of food costs—it was a pittance for the amount of work it took for her to put together a hot meal for between forty and one hundred people. Since prepping began before dawn, she typically earned less than $4 per hour. While she could have charged more, Ava said that cooking for such low pay was a way for her to demonstrate her commitment to Allah. At the same time, however, she relied on her Ramadan earnings to help supplement the less than $900 she received every month in SSI benefits. She had to balance her material needs with her spiritual hopes, a task that many in this urban community face.

Sympathizing with the poor as part of a religious community in which many members, if not most, are themselves struggling to make ends meet was often the hardest part of Ramadan at MAQ. Members agreed that it's their religious duty to feed the less fortunate, but what constitutes *lesser* fortune became a source of tension and debate each year. Some saw it as their duty to feed poor people in the neighborhood, regardless of religious affiliation. Others disagreed, arguing that fasting Muslims in need should eat first. The same tension extended to other forms of charity, such as distributing donated goods or money.[5] Resources—though more plentiful during this month than other times of the year—were still limited. As a community, believers had to work out who takes priority when there's not enough food, clothing, or money to go around. Should they feed fasting Muslims first? Or is the more pious act one of feeding a non-Muslim in need? Of the latter, should the masjid restrict access when a visitor seeking food is intoxicated? As we will see in this chapter, all are questions the believers at MAQ must work through in the course of trying to observe Islam's holiest month—a month that starts with excitement as believers prepare to deepen their faith, doing so within the local contours of life in South Central.

"Society Sees Us Fasting and Looking Better"

The weeks leading up to Ramadan signal that a new rhythm of daily life is on the horizon for believers, though when exactly it will start changes every year.⁶ Because Ramadan is based on a lunar calendar, it "moves up" annually by ten to eleven days.⁷ Muslims worldwide look to the night sky to determine when to start fasting, with a new moon signaling that the holy month has begun. Several factors can impede the sighting of the moon, such as rain or a cloudy night, and thus one must be ready to wait. This can make it difficult to plan, because the start of the fast also impacts when it will end. This means that the timing of the major celebration to conclude the month, Eid al-Fitr, is also often unknown.

Many Muslim Americans choose to start fasting when the Saudis do, with the belief that this is when the Prophet Muhammad would have begun his fast in Mecca; but for Imam Khalid and his supporters, it's important that the MAQ community decides the start of Ramadan based on a local sighting of the moon. This is one of many small ways in which MAQ's members engage Islam within the contours of local neighborhood life amid an air of defiance, pointedly ignoring or disagreeing with the actions of Muslims elsewhere in the world. Khalid makes the start of the fast official in consultation with other African American imams, who together go atop the roof of a nearby higher building in South Central to decide whether the moon can be seen.⁸ Once the sighting has been declared, masjid staff phone some of the regular attendees to alert them to the imams' ruling. These members then call others in their network, and eventually word spreads through the community. While younger members use social media, most participants at MAQ were older and preferred calling one another to share information. Inevitably, some don't get the word and instead start their fast one day earlier or later than others, while some refuse to listen to Khalid. Aisha's eldest son, Brother Asaad, was a good example of the latter action. He criticized Khalid's approach, finding that it didn't always correspond to what Asaad perceived as "proper" Islamic theology. If Asaad chose to start fasting one day earlier or later than others in the community (including his mother and siblings), it not only impacted whether he was fasting alone the first days of the holy month. It also meant that he would miss the Eid al-Fitr celebrations at the end of the month, because he still had fast days to complete. In this way, members could be defiant in how they engaged Islam with one another as well.

Not knowing exactly when the fast will start heightens the sense of excitement that surrounds Ramadan each year, an excitement that begins to build in the weeks leading up to the month. In the three or four Fridays beforehand, religious leaders shift the content of their khutbahs to discussions about fasting, intention, and piety. One year, Khalid's middle-aged protégé, imam Raqman Ahman, told believers they should acquire "an urge for natural foods" during Ramadan and that fasting should help with "sluggishness" and excess weight. Losing weight was one of the benefits believers looked forward to each year, with many under doctor's orders to get their weight down. They pointed out that their preference for eating a simple hot meal for iftar was more in line with the intent of the month, which was to seek purity in mind, body, and soul. I was told that people in Muslim-majority societies are more inclined to gain weight, because they stay up later eating heavy (often fried) foods. More than once, believers at MAQ commented to me that it was easier to observe Ramadan in places like Saudi Arabia and Egypt, where businesses often close during the day, thus limiting working hours.[9] Even here, though, believers creatively rewrite their struggle as religious minorities as one of deeper religious engagement that will lead to greater blessings, turning the act of fasting in a non-Muslim society into a process of outreach known as *dawah*. As Imam Ahman told believers, "Society sees us fasting and looking better and healthy. Then they begin to study for themselves and, *inshallah* [if Allah wills it], find Islam." But it's not just anyone in society that members of MAQ hope will find Islam. They focused their hopes on those most directly in their lives: people who live in South Central, as well as African American friends and family. The community has treated the neighborhood as its main recruitment ground since their origins in the Nation of Islam, when believers at MAQ first learned to frame Islam as a (defiant) force for good within the African American community. The irony, of course, is that the neighborhood is no longer majority African American and will probably never again reach the numbers of Black residents it once boasted.

Further nurturing a narrative that their pious actions stand as models for others is the self-discipline necessary to adjust their personal schedule during Ramadan, changes which help structure a different temporal landscape for the month.[10] Fasting disrupts routines and reorganizes daily patterns, making fasting "nothing less than a qualitative de-centering of everyday experience."[11] Believers rise before daybreak to eat while the rest of the neighborhood remains asleep. For those like Ava who lived with non-Muslim family, this can mean tiptoeing through the house to make the predawn meal *suhur* and offer Fajr, the first obligatory prayer of the day. Believers with formal employment may nap briefly or leave early to go to work, when their energy is highest. As the day progresses, they feel the physiological effects of fasting—sluggishness, glassy eyes, and bad breath. Brother Naeem worked as an administrator at a nearby public high school and seemed especially self-conscious about how parents, students, and other non-Muslims would interpret his "changed breath." The many more in the community who were either self-employed or living off a fixed income adjusted their daytime routine to budget the time needed to shop, cook, and prepare for the evening's rituals. When I could, I followed some of the sisters during the day, finding that most of their "free" time was spent scouring supermarkets and halal butchers for good deals on food for their families and the masjid. When I wasn't able to tag along, informal in situ interviews at night allowed me to see that they frequently visited two or more stores in a day to seek out the lowest advertised prices in local circulars. It was one of the many strategies believers relied on to keep costs down during a month when they expected to give more to the mosque.

"Ain't No Circulating or Goin' Nowhere"

When not at work or running errands, believers try to limit themselves to home and the masjid. At MAQ, this change in routine was especially visible at night, when the mosque transformed into a hub of social activity. Sharing in this activity strengthens the sense of religious community amid the secular environment. Community building takes place year-round, of course, but the ways in which believers summon one another toward a particular kind of local Muslim identification is most visible during Ramadan because of the concerted effort members make to attach themselves to MAQ.

Believers start to arrive at the masjid just before sunset, though a few tend to arrive earlier so they can read the Qur'an inside the quiet prayer hall. At the sound of the *adhan* (call to prayer), they break their fast with a simple selection of fruit, dates, and water, served on plastic serving platters placed on tables scattered around the yard. A full meal will come later, after the obligatory Maghrib prayer just after sunset. With little conversation, believers eat the slices of precut watermelon, suck the juice out of orange wedges, or reach for a bottle of water, making sure to consume in moderation.

When Maghrib prayer begins, typically fewer than ten women are inside the sisters' section of the prayer hall, including one or two young women or girls. The brothers' side will be fuller, with at least twenty making the first prayer each night. More believers will show up for dinner, coming to eat and then retreating to their homes or rooms once the meal is over. It's not uncommon during Ramadan for Muslim men (and some women) who live in single-room-occupancy hotels and halfway houses around Skid Row to make the twenty-minute bus ride from downtown Los Angeles to MAQ to get a free home-cooked meal. Brothers and sisters on parole tend to leave the masjid earlier because of strict curfews, making it hard for them to complete all the Taraweeh prayers—additional prayers performed after the nighttime Isha prayer during Ramadan—in summer months when darkness descends later. They also can't socialize in the hours after official services end.

Sisters Ava and Aisha, by contrast, developed a reputation for remaining at the masjid well past prayer time and into the early morning hours. Sometimes, Ava would sleep the remainder of the night in the prayer hall or in her van in the masjid parking lot under the protective gaze of the brothers who lived on site. She said she needed some peace from her non-Muslim family, including the three adult siblings with whom she lived in their late mother's house eleven blocks from MAQ. It was part of Ava's everyday battle to get her siblings to respect her religious practices, which she managed through a mix of tears, laughter, and cussing. Most of the time, the living arrangement was bearable if annoying to her; during the fast, however, she found it additionally burdensome to live under the same roof with people who didn't share her Muslim faith. It was common for me to hear believers say they were avoiding their non-Muslim family during Ramadan, ignoring missed phone calls and turning down invitations to family gatherings. The masjid became a second home for many, a halal island to escape to during Ramadan. The irony in all this is that members want their loved ones to find Islam as a path toward righteousness. In addition, they see their deeper religious engagement during Ramadan as serving their *dawah* efforts, though they're experiencing heightened differences with their immediate and extended family members.

Amplifying believers' struggles as religious-racial minorities was the neighborhood's status as a majority Latino space, where people were not only eating and drinking throughout the day but doing so as they consumed a variety of pork and alcohol products in public view. To make traversing a non-Muslim landscape more manageable, believers sought to limit their movements in the neighborhood and applied the same edict to their children. I was talking with Sister Haleema one night when her teenage granddaughter asked to go to Walgreens and then out to meet friends. Haleema told her no, saying, "Ain't no circulating or goin' nowhere." For Haleema and other believers, Ramadan is a time for forming good habits, which is harder to do when running around the neighborhood with non-Muslims. She allowed her granddaughter to be out late, but only if she kept to the masjid. This emphasis on avoiding social activities with people who aren't fasting was partly pragmatic. Much of our contemporary social lives revolves around eating and drinking with others, so during Ramadan, when observant Muslims avoid going out to eat or attending nonreligious gatherings, they'll necessarily interact less with people outside the faith. The emphasis on avoiding social activities with people who aren't fasting was also symbolic and part of a concerted effort to reinforce shared religious identities.

All the ways in which believers engage Islam during Ramadan are part of a rhythm of social life that creates a distinct experiential pattern for one-twelfth of each year. What made this pattern so evocative in summoning MAQ's members into a stronger religious identification was how "arrhythmic" it was with the rhythms of the neighborhood in which they and their families lived.[12] These contrasting patterns of social life reinforced their perceptions of a distinct Muslim din inside the gates of the masjid and a less righteous life outside on the streets of South Central. Similar to their dealings with Christian relatives during Islam's holiest month, believers experience a mix of competing forces: they are pulled by religious obligation to focus on helping the less fortunate in the immediate neighborhood, yet they are pushed by a desire for righteousness to disassociate from people they deem *of* the hood.

"Wish We Could Do Ramadan All the Time"

No activity in the rhythm of life during Ramadan evoked the push-pull connection between MAQ and its neighborhood as strongly as the iftar dinner, which I attended more than 120 times over the years. More than any other activity I observed at the mosque, iftar offered members of this minority faith an opportunity to strengthen their religious engagement while reaffirming their commitment to community. Food is a frequent and integral component of many ritual activities associated with spiritual fellowship.[13] Eating at the mosque creates an obvious social pressure to observe the fast in a society in which most people aren't Muslim, but, more important, believers said it offers them a chance to connect with one another.[14] As Imam Khalid said to believers, "If your family's not here, come. . . . [It's] important we maintain family connections and relationships"—the obvious implication of his words being that the masjid community should be family during Islam's holy month. This is the kind of civic action that bonds individuals with "a kind of sociological superglue" and creates in-group loyalty.[15]

The night of my first iftar, Brother Naeem pointed to the tables of believers and said, "It's beautiful. This is the socialization part, and it will only get bigger as time goes on." For believers like Naeem, who couldn't attend jumah because of work in another part of the city, iftar was sometimes the only weekday activity they could participate in at MAQ. Sisters expressed a similar feeling of joy, with one laughing and saying to me, "Wish we could do Ramadan all the time. I think that's what Allah is working us to. . . . It's the bomb! The men be falling on each other and huggin'." These positive perceptions of the "socialization" that iftar promises contributed to an overall feeling of excitement in the lead-up to and first days of Ramadan.

The communality needed to organize iftar furthers the excitement. Before the start of fasting, members sign up on a dry-erase board to sponsor a night. Then the sponsor cooks at home, cooks at the masjid, or hires someone to cook for him or her, typically a sister in the community who works as a caterer or cook (like Ava). Masjid staff want the food ready well before sunset so that they and a select group of volunteers can be ready to serve immediately after Maghrib. As the believers leave the prayer hall they organize themselves into one line segregated by gender, with women served first. They move through the food line cafeteria style along a row of long tables under a portable tent, directing servers, who wear disposable plastic aprons and latex gloves, as to what they want on their plate. Believers then take their plate to one of the half-dozen picnic tables scattered throughout the property to eat in quiet conversation, often though not always continuing to segregate themselves by gender.

Since the members of MAQ usually ate outside, they could hear what was going on in the streets around us: sirens, "ghetto birds" (police helicopters), cars blasting rap music, houses blasting mariachi music. There was also a Pentecostal storefront church down the street with an excellent PA system, and almost every night the pastor got on his microphone to shout biblical declarations and prophesies in a mix of English and Spanish. All these sounds became worked into believers' conversations, providing audio cues that sparked talk about the neighborhood. And it was in these conversations that they reinforced to one another the symbolic boundaries they had constructed between their community and residents of the neighborhood around them. Over dinner one Ramadan, Sister Aisha said, "I thank Allah that all of my kids stayed Muslim . . . and that none of them went to jail!" I told her that was no small thing given the statistics on mass incarceration, and she shouted, "Yes! They are from, you know, the hood, but not *of* the hood." Aisha's desire to portray her family as different from (and better than) people who were "of the hood" fit within a larger framework of identity construction at MAQ in which believers sought to symbolically distance themselves from the problems and stigmas associated with living and worshipping in a low-income inner-city neighborhood.

In an ethnographic study of a religious district in Boston, Omar McRoberts found that many Black urban churchgoers were not often residents of the depressed neighborhoods where they worshipped.[16] Instead, they commuted in on Sundays to attend services, the location of the church more a result of cheap rent than proximity to home. This meant that congregants had little to no attachment to the neighborhood and often strove to position themselves "over and against the street."[17] By contrast, many believers at MAQ lived either in the immediate area, like Aisha and Ava, or in a nearby portion of South Central, like Naeem. They saw the street as part of their ordinary lives, weaving understandings of the neighborhood—and sometimes reinforcing stereotypes about it—into their conceptions of religious identity. This was clear to me one night in 2008. I was sitting with a large group when Brother Naeem announced that another brother at the table had his car broken into while visiting a different South Central mosque the previous night. The men then discussed who might be responsible for the theft, focusing on two prominent Black gangs.

Naeem asked, "Sixty-sixes?"

"No," Brother Saddiq responded. "Van Ness Gangsters."

"Same thing," Naeem said. "Maggots."

Naeem's use of the term *maggots* to describe local gangs captures the strong sense of moral superiority this community of mostly older African Americans felt when comparing themselves to others in the neighborhood, including other African Americans. This symbolic boundary making took Aisha's dichotomous framing of being "from" but not "of" the hood further, marking others in the neighborhood as pests (and a particularly detested kind).

Naeem regularly used colorful language to express disapproval, but the sentiment that gangs are a neighborhood nuisance was commonly shared among believers. They frequently invoked the term *ghetto* as an adjective to refer to people in the neighborhood who sold or did drugs, dressed provocatively, loitered, acted brashly, or exhibited other behaviors traditionally associated with negative stereotypes of poor urban neighborhoods. Such behaviors are supposed to occur "out there" in the profane world of South Central, a kind of religious mapping reminiscent of McRoberts's study.[18] In that study, the street was more than a physical place in that it also formed a trope to which churchgoers assigned different meanings that helped them decide what it means to be religious. The way that clergy in McRoberts's study made sense of the pious person's place in a morally corrupt urban environment also evoked a frame of being "in but not of," though in the case of the Christian churches of Boston's Four Corners neighborhood, the frame evoked a more metaphysical dilemma of "the irony of faith in an apparently faithless world."[19] This frame was easier to employ because most church members didn't live in the area. Believers at MAQ had an additional incentive as residents of a stigmatized neighborhood to create a symbolic separation from non-Muslim residents, whom outsiders may not be able to distinguish from members of the mosque. This tension was most pronounced during the time of pious renewal and strengthening that Ramadan constitutes.

"We Serve the Community First"

Given believers' efforts to symbolically separate themselves from the people they perceived as "of the hood," I expected them to work even harder during the holiest Islamic month to push for a physical separation. So it was striking during my first Ramadan at MAQ to see members invite the very people whom they strove to distance themselves from to come inside the masjid to receive a plate at iftar, including suspected gang members, sex workers, and addicts. Their action highlights that during Ramadan, part of living one's faith in the MAQ community is constituted through interaction with the neighborhood. What's more, believers fed guests first, sometimes at the expense of being able to feed fasting Muslims. If someone walked in from the street, a member of the mosque's security team or a nearby believer shouted "Guest!" and ushered the visitor to the front of the line. Brother Naeem, who directed the serving line, explained, "We serve the community first, then elder sisters and sisters, then kids, then the elder brothers and us [brothers]." In Naeem's explanation, "the community" means the neighborhood, the people ushered to the front of the line. I found that when believers engaged in charity work, they treated the larger community as one based on place, not faith. This practice shifted the process of becoming religious into one shaped through identification *with* the neighborhood, not in opposition to it.[20]

Such frame switching means that believers have charted a moral cartography that allows boundary flexing. Depending on the situation, they may tense a boundary like a muscle, to show strength. But when it serves a higher purpose, such as fulfilling a religious obligation or maintaining racial pride, believers relax that boundary. Importantly, most of the guests joining the serving line are also Black, meaning that believers have created a racially inclusive but religiously distinct space. This boundary flexing allows them to maintain symbolic distance with neighborhood elements they deem *haram* (forbidden) without sacrificing an attachment to the history of South Central as a place of pride for African American culture.

Turning one's gaze to people in the immediate urban environment in order to earn blessings from Allah was part of the spirit of Ramadan at MAQ, with believers explaining that the practice of feeding passersby has roots in the time of the Prophet Muhammad. And it was a major source of pride to provide a "spread" every night as proof of a socially conscious Islam. Yet it was no small feat. Members of MAQ are far from wealthy, and only a small proportion of the regular attendees could afford the $80–$120 it cost to sponsor an iftar. With between forty and sixty people expected every night, the meal, roughly $2–$3 per head, consisted of the same basic combination most nights: a piece of baked chicken or fried fish, a scoop of white rice, a small iceberg lettuce salad, and maybe a side of bean soup or canned green beans. Believers prided themselves on being able to provide this spread every night of Ramadan, having done so for decades. They pointed out that many communities offer dinner only on weekends or during the last ten days of the fast, including other mosques in South Central as well as larger Islamic centers. At one of the moderately sized Arab-run mosques in LA, it cost a minimum of $1,400 to sponsor one iftar.[21]

Organizing a fresh, hot meal for sixty people is not easy, and doing so with abundant resources for thirty days straight would prove stressful. For those on a tight budget, it becomes a true feat that tests endurance and patience—especially after an eighteen-hour day of fasting. Believers could have pointed to their limited resources as justification to limit whom they fed while still fulfilling their religious obligations, with several strands of Islamic thought backing up just such a claim. Historically speaking, in Muslim societies "large-scale demonstrations of generosity" during Ramadan are common, but it's most often wealthy Muslims who "set tables that accommodate whole neighborhoods and welcome passersby for the iftar meal to break the fast."[22] Sponsorship of meals is not a strict obligation, and even today the practice tends to occur among "practicing Muslims of rank and wealth."[23]

However, believers at MAQ rejected the idea that only the wealthy are obligated to feed the poor and instead stressed that every Muslim is obliged to help the less fortunate. Feeding people in the neighborhood was a constitutive component of how believers fulfilled their zakat. In doing so, neighborhood outreach during Ramadan allowed members to incorporate their own material hardship into formulations of a more moral self. Sister Fatima worked as a cashier at a local grocery store, raising her children and helping care for grandchildren on her own after a difficult divorce. She joked one night about Ramadan, "I'm po'! Take the *o* and the *r* off. It's *po*'!" Then she turned more serious: "You can always give one percent. One percent of anything is not much. . . . Even if you have five dollars, give a nickel." This, Fatima explained, signals your *intent*.

Making Good Intentions

Intentions are crucial to believers during Ramadan and afterward, and they must demonstrate rightful intent before proceeding with any ritual or act in order for Allah to accept it. Even if an action doesn't take place, a believer may point to the existence of intention as proof of rightfulness.[24] In some Muslim courts, a legal claim may be considered valid based primarily on intention.[25] "We are not responsible for the consequences of our actions, but we are responsible for making the commitment," Imam Khalid preached one Friday. He taught that a person cannot force something to happen, because only Allah can; but, *inshallah*, a believer can commit to try. Part of the spirit of Ramadan is to intend to do more, to build up one's religious intentions on both an individual level—committing to pray more, for example—and on a social level—increasing charity, a primary means.

Of course, intending to do something and doing it aren't identical. Leaders pointed out that it isn't enough to say you intend to do well because, according to Imam Khalid, religion is like soap: "Only works when we use it." Following his direction and that of the late national African American leader Imam W. D. Mohammed, believers attending MAQ learned to see intentions as a blueprint to craft action. Trying to do what Allah wants *is* the path to righteousness, and it's one that becomes the spoken road of desire for members during Ramadan. We see this not only in how members increase the intensity and frequency of worship but also, and perhaps even more important, in how they work together to feed the less fortunate in the neighborhood. They use these actions as proof to the divine (Allah) of their rightful intention.

Social scientists generally consider intention part of the "interior" of the self; an individual's motivations and desires are not considered accessible to observation. As such, rarely does interactionist thought give attention to the intent of an action—focus instead goes almost exclusively to consequences. Such a perspective limits conceptions of agency, however, holding it hostage to a limited and, in the context of religious agency, Christian way of thinking. Anthropologist Saba Mahmood makes this point in her book about the women's mosque movement in Egypt. Mahmood urges scholars to analyze agency "within the grammar of concepts within which it resides."[26] This requires "that the concept of agency . . . be delinked from the goal of progressive politics," thereby freeing us to see agency through the lens of the people engaging religion.[27] In Islam, ethics is an embodied practice that lives through a relation to the divine, thereby requiring a different notion of subject-formation than dominant epistemologies allow. Intentionality is the language through which believers at MAQ convey hope for action and thus set themselves up to enact agency. The goal in making good intentions is to cultivate a more moral self by strengthening one's din; this is done not to resist external sources of power but to work toward pleasing the ultimate higher power. We must look at what believers say they intend to do and why, as well as where their intentions go unfulfilled, to understand how and why believers act as they do.

Treating intentions as a core component of agency requires a departure also from how social scientists tend to conceive of religion among marginalized populations. When they write about how people in poverty draw from religion to deal with hardship, religion is often dismissed as an opiate, a way of keeping "the oppressed pacified and blind to the injustice of their circumstances."[28] Though they may be politically sympathetic to the struggles of religious minorities, most social scientists are less likely to see religion as a solution to hardship, pointing instead to material solutions. Believers at MAQ, by contrast, see Islam as their framework for a better future. It's not that they can't see structural problems. They know better than most how racism and poverty have stripped them of opportunities. However, they also find life to be about more than their material conditions, with belief motivating them to move toward something deeper, more existential in character.

As a sociologist, I am trained to see the root causes of believers' problems as structurally produced. Yet I also know that an emphasis on structural forces tends to obscure the varied modalities of moral action that people in marginalized urban spaces enact. An overemphasis on structure can turn people's responses to hardship into little more than adaptations.[29] As Sudhir Venkatesh notes, "The complexity within, and differentiations among, the range of processes that are captured in the catch-all category of adaptation (and its analytic synonyms: adjustment, response, substitution, etc.) becomes erased as quickly as they are gathered together within this single analytic trope."[30] The trope of adaptation cannot grasp the creative ways in which believers at MAQ construct a Muslim "way of life" *in conjunction with* their social positioning as believers located in an environment at once hostile toward Islam and a powerful force for constructing a more pious self. Standard definitions of *agency* as "coping" or "adaptation" also cannot capture the complexity in how MAQ's members articulate their goals, hopes, and dreams. The goal is not to close off the possibilities but instead to see the ways that believers strive. Believers wanted to improve their socioeconomic conditions, but they also strove to engage Islam in ways that further a sense of religious self in direct connection with the neighborhood, not over or against it. In other words, it wasn't enough to cultivate the self; one also had to engage with others.

Standing at the microphone on the eve of Ramadan one year, Imam Khalid told believers, "Every day we are challenged during the fast. [But] Islam doesn't believe in isolation. *Our test is living a community life.*" This test was at the heart of what it meant to live a Muslim way of life in South Central. When believers reached out to neighbors and problems ensued, as the remainder of the chapter illustrates, efforts to enact good intentions enabled the cultivation of a deeper social piety. It is in examining how believers work through their struggles with the neighborhood together as a collective, and in conflict with one another, that we can begin to appreciate the sage warning Imam Khalid gave: that the test of Ramadan is living a community life.

"We're Getting Some Hard-Core Neighbors"

One night, I heard a voice calling for assistance at the mosque gate, where I found a middle-aged woman I recognized as one of the sex workers in the neighborhood. The woman asked me to bring her a plate, because she didn't want to offend the people inside with her short skirt and low-cut top. She wouldn't have been turned away had she gone inside the property dressed as she was. I had seen plenty of women in less clothing being served, including a woman wearing a thin, short nightgown who left with extra food and even some donated clothing. While it's possible that the woman at the gate didn't feel welcome—religious organizations on Skid Row are well known for demanding certain codes of behavior from those seeking social services—her attendance the previous few nights dressed in less provocative clothing suggested a reverence for believers' religious leanings.[31]

Interactions with guests fed a narrative among believers that neighborhood non-Muslims respected MAQ members' strong moral codes. Displays of deference reaffirmed believers' collective sense of moral superiority in the neighborhood as well as the notion that African American Muslims are intimidating in a righteous manner. Brothers went to great lengths to be chivalrous toward female guests, and though they were harsher with male guests, the latter usually displayed deference nonetheless. Young men pulled up their sagging pants when Naeem barked at them to do so, and guests with open bottles and cans of alcohol left their drinks outside when asked. On a night in 2012 when the number of guests was especially high, Naeem leaned into the microphone to joke, "Oh, we doin' some *dawah*. I mean, we're getting some hard-core neighbors, and they're staying and eating with us." A few believers laughed. Naeem added, "Some of them smell like things they shouldn't be doing, but don't kill them!" That joke drew more laughter. It was part of a larger narrative—perpetuated mostly by brothers—that the masjid serves an important organizing role in the neighborhood thanks to the community's past in the Nation of Islam, when Fruit of Islam soldiers patrolled local streets instilling order.

Rather than causing fear, feeding guests during Ramadan created a sense of safety at MAQ. I saw this most clearly in interactions between longtime members and the men who worked at a popular bodega across the street. The believers thought the men were gang members and the bodega their front for a drug-dealing operation, but didn't worry about becoming victims of possible connected violence.[32] I wondered how they came to have such a friendly relationship with a group of suspected drug dealers, and then I saw interactions between them and these men during Ramadan.

The young men (mostly Latino) and their older African American leader, a man with curly reddish hair whom believers knew only as "Red," would line up for a plate at iftar. Red taught the younger men to step back to allow the Muslim women to pass by without possible physical contact, and he snapped at his men when they cursed in front of believers. Red, whom believers described as an "OG" (Original Gangster), also gave the Muslim greeting to members (As-salaam alaikum [Peace be unto you]) and often placed a dollar or two in the zakat basket. When doing so, he even copied believers' words, saying, "Here's a ducat for the bucket." The ways in which men from the bodega went out of their way to demonstrate respect perpetuated MAQ's institutional legacy as a moral fortress.

Of course, no symbolic boundary is fixed or immutable. All boundaries are processual and achieved via interactions in which the self is (re)produced by a constant process of identification in relation to others. In such a phenomenological approach, believers can "consciously or subconsciously expect a certain interactional unfolding of the situation," but they can't control its outcome.[33] Though believers want their guests to display deference, the latter act within a different cultural framework and thus may not adhere to the same standards of behavior as fasting Muslims. When members let down the drawbridge during Ramadan to invite the very people they perceive as their "hard-core neighbors," opportunities open up for potentially problematic interactions. In situations where a guest didn't observe mosque norms, tensions could develop over the most Islamic way to respond. These tensions occurred less frequently between believers and guests than *among believers*, as the following vignette from my field notes demonstrates:

A disheveled man in tattered pants, face streaked with dirt, stumbles through the wrought-iron gate onto the property, trailed by a similarly unkempt man. Some of the clean-shaven men in collared button-down shirts look up at the man they know as Chester, but others seem too tired to bother. Chester's friend follows him inside and the two begin to reenact a scene, with Chester pulling his friend's arms behind his back and slapping on invisible handcuffs. Chester is slurring his words as he pretends to arrest the other man. The two men laugh, throwing their heads back. Their chatter momentarily disrupts the calm of the masjid, and a few moments later the men settle at a picnic table outside.

Chester seems restless and barely two minutes pass before he is up again, moving toward a long empty table. This close to sunset, the food should be here. but believers are still waiting for the pans of chicken, rice, and bean soup. Brother Fareed, the seventy-four-year-old masjid treasurer, dressed in powder-blue suit and wide necktie, yells at the approaching Chester, "Get back!" When Chester stumbles back to the picnic table, he has trouble figuring out how to pull his legs over the bench to sit. He stands with one foot on the bench, prompting Sister Haleema to snap, "Turn around and get your foot off! You're making the seat dirty!"

"Allahumma inni laka sumtu wa bika aamantu wa alayka tawakkaltu wa ala rizq-ika-aftartu." At these words announcing the end of the day's fasting, the silent women and men slowly crowd around two smaller side tables to feast on sliced oranges and Medjoon dates. Chester and his friend remain at the picnic table. Believers then move inside for prayer. When they finish and return outside, the food still isn't there. It's now dark, and more guests have come in from the nearby streets. They cluster at the edge of the parking lot away from the believers.

A car turns into the gravel lot, and Brother Khalifah hurriedly exits from the driver side, opening the side doors to several men who have rushed toward the car to help. The men transfer half a dozen large silver pans to the long table. Brother Fareed tells me to grab a soup ladle from the kitchen, and when I return, Chester is slumped over on the ground. From behind me I hear someone explain, "He tripped on the cord" (referring to the floodlight clamped to the tent). Chester struggles to get back up, relying on the aid of two men from the masjid, who prop him up with their shoulders and move him over to the crowd of guests at the opposite side of the property.

Just then, Brother Malcolm marches forward, shouting, "Get him out of here! He's drunk!" Before Malcolm can reach Chester, though, Brother Elijah navigates between the men, yelling at Malcolm to stop. Elijah grabs Chester by his coat sleeve and tries to pull him back toward the masjid.

Malcolm shouts, "He's drunk! He shouldn't be up there near people!"

Elijah snaps back, "It don't matter! You don't treat no one that way! He's hungry!"

Another brother comes over to plead with Malcolm to calm down, but he won't. Malcolm hollers back, "He's not Muslim!"

"No," Elijah responds bitterly, "*You're* a Muslim!" After he calls Malcolm a "savage," Sister Haleema pleads with the men to stop. All the while, Chester looks oblivious to the scuffle. He smiles and chuckles as he sways between the men. Only when someone brings Chester a plate and he leaves the property do Malcolm and Elijah back down.

Tensions continued the next day at a preplanned community meeting. Imam Khalid said, "We had a brother came here last night that they tell me he was drunk. What do we do? We feed him!" The imam joked that the man was sober enough to find the masjid, so it could be hoped that someday he'll be sober enough to find Allah, generating a few chuckles among the audience. Khalid used his religious authority to reinforce a policy of feeding guests that Brother Naeem had implemented and Brother Elijah had forcefully argued to maintain, but one that also conflicted with what others in the community felt to be Islamically appropriate.

The incident with Chester captures exactly the kind of interactional dilemma that believers face trying to reach out to others in an environment where drug and alcohol addicts can (and do) wander in from the street. It was a problem pastors complained of in McRoberts's study of Black storefront churches and one that seemed to reinforce congregants' desires to symbolically and physically separate their religious communities from the evil of the street.[34] But recall Imam Khalid's declaration that "Islam doesn't believe in isolation." Part of the very spirit of Ramadan is to try to connect with the divine by sympathizing with the less fortunate. How one achieves this was not always as clear-cut as believers professed in the lead-up to Ramadan.

The argument between Malcolm and Elijah underscores the varied ways of reaching out to others in need even within this single small community: Malcolm believed it wrong to serve someone who was drunk, while Elijah believed it to be the obligation of Muslims to serve anyone in need. How do we make sense of the men's different interpretations of what it means to be a Muslim? Conventional sociological approaches tell us to look for variables to account for difference, such as race, class, occupation, educational attainment, and neighborhood residence. Yet in comparing the men by traditional measures, they appear more alike than different. Both men were Black and underemployed. They were of similar ages and religious backgrounds, having come through the Nation of Islam decades earlier before transitioning to Sunni Islam. They were both "old heads" from the neighborhood.[35] The friends even lived next door to each other in a small apartment complex a few miles from MAQ, allowing Elijah to rely on Malcolm for rides to the masjid when his van broke down. So what accounts for their dispute? The tension is best explained by their shared determination to undertake a moral project rubbing against their varied interpretations of what *moral* means in this setting. Morality here becomes a kind of social currency, used to acquire status. The more the men put into their din, the more they had at stake to defend it.

In communities where people are more alike than different and where more common markers of success are out of reach, morality can sometimes be the only boundary left to cultivate a sense of worth. Jennifer Sherman reached that conclusion after a year spent living in a logging town on the remote edges of Northern California which saw its economic livelihood decimated by changing environmental laws.[36] She found that with few jobs and little wealth, residents employed a moral framework to situate themselves as worthy, upstanding citizens in the face of changing structural and cultural conditions. "Morality has slowly become the force underlying these old divisions," she explains. "It has also provided them with new definitions of success and failure and new avenues to achieving the American dream in the absence of so many of the more common status markers found throughout American society."[37] In other words, morality becomes *the* axis of difference when there are no other forms of distinction available.

Understanding the incident with Chester as one in which believers competed for moral status also requires attention to gender. While it was a brother (Malcolm) who disagreed with the edict to feed guests regardless of their behavior, women at MAQ complained more often than men about the practice. Later in the same month, Sister Aisha decided she was fed up with the smell of alcohol on guests' breaths and how they stumbled around the property when coming in for food. Even though guests rarely stayed, preferring to take their plate to the curb to eat, Aisha insisted that they not come near the women. She took it upon herself to create a separate serving table for guests, arriving early at the mosque, filling Styrofoam containers with cooked food, and stacking them on a folding table in the parking lot about ten feet from the main serving line. She wanted guests to grab a takeaway container without coming into contact with fasting believers. Aisha told me later that she and Naeem had gotten into an argument over this, but she was determined to ignore the "hardheaded" brother. I heard a few sisters comment privately that they liked the separate line, but tellingly, no one helped Aisha and after a few days she stopped setting it up. She tried to revive the practice a couple of years later with the aid of another agitated sister, but once more it failed to last more than a few days.

Naeem could limit Aisha's actions in part because men held a monopoly on formal positions of religious authority at MAQ. However, even formal power has its limits, particularly when resources are limited. Such was the case in 2008, when the nationwide financial crisis further squeezed an already tight Ramadan budget. Better-off members who worked for local and state public agencies saw their individual incomes constrained by furloughs, and donations to the mosque decreased as a result of personal belt-tightening. There were several nights when the men at the end of the line weren't able to eat or received less food than those served first. In these moments, the only resource left was a sense of moral worth, as this excerpt from my field notes captures well:

More guests walk up to the line, but Naeem tells them the masjid is out of food. The men wait a moment, then see the picked-over aluminum trays before heading back to the street. An emaciated Black man with white hair, tight stained jeans, oversized coat, and tennis shoes too small to fit around his bare heels emerges behind the group of existing guests. He lingers in the parking lot, unable to stand still. Naeem notices the man and motions for him to come over to the table. Naeem scrounges up a last and final plate, giving it to the man. A few minutes later, Naeem sits down at our table, eating just a piece of bread and some dates. He comments to Sister Haleema that he would rather give his plate to a guest. She offers her extra plate (she usually saves one or two to take home), but he says no. Naeem adds, "I really appreciate it, but I'm fine." Then he says there is a "prison mentality" tonight, and a sister at the table vigorously nods her head yes. Encouraged, Naeem continues, "The brothers came through and ate and then went back for seconds, even though guests were still coming for food. . . . [They're] buzzards."

Naeem avoided the food because he said he didn't want people to "put that spirit in me." He also came late the next several nights, skipping iftar and attending only Isha and Taraweeh prayers. The men that Naeem identified as "buzzards" did not bring out a sense of moral superiority the way that neighborhood guests did. Rather, the presence of a "prison mentality" within the community dampened Naeem's overall enthusiasm about Ramadan, which just days before he had called beautiful. He may have been trying to demonstrate his Islamic worth by going without food, but it came at the expense of his feeling detached from fellow fasting Muslims.

"That Ain't Right, and I Told Him"

Some years it was Brother Naeem who retreated; other years he tried to prevent others from retreating. At the microphone after Isha prayer one night in 2013, he said, "Let's not be discouraged by small numbers. Let's keep doing what we're doing." It was unusual to bring direct attention to low participation at Masjid al-Quran, and his comment prompted looks of confusion among the sisters. Thinking I may have missed something, I asked a woman sitting near me why Naeem said this. Sister Natalie explained that the mosque had had a food giveaway the previous morning. She said the man who donated the uncooked food—a South Asian from a wealthier Muslim community—used to deliver the boxes to the homes of elderly believers in South Central, generally recognized as the Muslims most in need. But the South Asian brother had called Natalie and said that the number of elderly and underprivileged believers had become too great for him to make individual deliveries this year, so their boxes would instead need be picked up at Masjid al-Quran. According to Natalie, the mosque was supposed to set aside boxes for the Muslims on the list before giving away the rest, only "Naeem messed it up," she said, and gave the food away to non-Muslims first. She told me it was just like the times during iftar when Naeem let the guys from the bodega or people coming from known crack houses get in the front of the line. "They be lit up," she said, yet he would usher them to front of the line. "That ain't right, and I told him."

Natalie shared that she had "heart palpitations" after waiting hours in the heat and not knowing whether she would get her box. Since retiring as a teacher at the mosque's former Islamic school, she had subsisted on a government-assisted fixed income. She was well into her eighties at the time of the food giveaway, and it took several days for her to recover from the dramatic event. Sister Ava, who was listening in, told us she had gone to a giveaway earlier in the month. "It was *bad*," she said, with people from the neighborhood showing up drunk that morning and then getting irate because they had to wait. On both occasions, people were told to arrive at nine o'clock, but the delivery truck hadn't shown up until after noon.

The following weekend, I went to a giveaway. I promised Sister Natalie that I would get a box and deliver it to her apartment. I arrived just after eleven o'clock, knowing from my contacts in the masjid office that the truck wouldn't arrive until noon. As I drove up, I saw seven women and men sitting under the tent and a few others lined up outside the closed gate. The women inside the gate wore head coverings, while the women outside wore shorts and sleeveless shirts—a clue as to who was an insider and who was not. I settled on the steps of the women's entrance to observe. Several more hours passed before I had Natalie's box in hand. I had to wait for the late truck and then through the ensuing chaos. The South Asian brother driving the truck wasn't sure how to distribute the boxes, and the brothers at MAQ quarreled over who should lead. Brothers Malcolm and Sulayman yelled at each other; Naeem yelled at everyone. Dozens of Muslims showed up who didn't attend MAQ but had been told to go there for their promised boxes. Meanwhile, people on the street were shouting through the gate, complaining about their treatment. I became so frustrated at one point that I left, but as I pulled my car out of the gate I felt guilty and turned around to wait for my friend's box.

What was in the box that caused Sister Natalie to experience heart palpitations? Two uncooked chickens, an uncooked roast, a bag of rice, a bottle of corn oil, and a box of dates—food that I dropped off to the one-bedroom apartment she shared with her granddaughter. The notoriously stern former teacher was so overcome with gratitude, she uncharacteristically hugged me. Amid my shock at receiving this one and only hug in more than five years of knowing Natalie, I began to formulate a clearer picture of the role of religious institutions in the fight against poverty.

The literature on civic religion portrays institutions like MAQ as "voluntary organizations," because no laws require participation in them. Members' involvement in such organizations is thought to enhance their civic skills and political participation, a perspective dating to Alexis de Tocqueville's famed account of American democracy. However, in looking at the needs of members like Sister Natalie, we might question how voluntary MAQ has become for believers who struggle to make ends meet and rely on their faith community for basic needs, such as food. These struggles have intensified for believers like Natalie amid their constricting social world. They are striving to create a Muslim community nested within the larger South Central community, but the larger community is no longer majority Black or African American. With fewer family and friends living nearby to whom she can turn to construct the support systems that once defined the everyday experience of Black women and men in urban environments, Natalie has come to rely on the Muslim community for greater support and survival.[38] Her struggles then become part of the worship experience, as is the case for other Muslim women and men in need. But resources are few, and this creates competition among believers for both material and moral worth that can threaten internal bonds.

The strain of a religious community made up of people in need trying to sympathize with the "less" fortunate in their neighborhood brings into focus the limits of believers' good intentions. Believers wanted to help struggling neighbors in and around the community. They saw it as their Islamic duty, that to be a good Muslim requires showing sympathy by fasting and feeding the poor. Believers displayed this sympathetic orientation to the street while regarding themselves as morally superior to others in the neighborhood, taking on the image of a "caring self" in constructing notions of what is right as Muslims.[39] This cultivation of a caring self-image was an essential component of how the MAQ community acquired its own perceptions of status. But how to translate good intentions into successful strategies of action wasn't straightforward in moments of scarcity. At times, the needs of the neighborhood strained available mosque resources. Some believers responded by pushing for further separation from the non-Muslim poor around them, while others thought it more Islamically appropriate to feed the neediest regardless of religious identification or perceptions of moral deservingness. The conflicts that emerged during the distribution of zakat also revealed that the boundary believers constructed between themselves and others in the neighborhood was more porous than it first appeared. They wanted to see themselves as better off because of their faith, but it wasn't always clear that they were. Conflicts exposed internal systems of hierarchy, leaving believers like Sister Natalie with a negative view of her wealthier Muslim brother who could afford to leave the mosque without taking a box of food. Meanwhile, the more affluent within the community, like Naeem, felt a different kind of spirit intruding on their Ramadan when they viewed fellow Muslims as prioritizing personal hardship over religious ends.

*   *   *

Though it seemed straightforward from MAQ members' conversations leading up to Ramadan that they knew what it means to make good intentions, their enacting religious goals together presented the kind of challenges that can tear at the social fabric of community life. The struggles believers encounter when working through different interpretations of intentionality remind us that "agency contextualizes and makes visible structural conditions."[40] The struggle to sustain the spirit of Ramadan that arose from competition over finite resources suggests that the moral distinction believers tried to construct between themselves and what they perceived as those "in the hood" wasn't impenetrable, at least not in a community where members themselves struggled. The strains of trying to sympathize with others in need coupled with the disagreements that arose over how to enact an ethos of collective empathy put into greater perspective the warnings Imam Khalid and other religious leaders gave each Ramadan on the eve of fasting, when they reminded believers that the test of Ramadan "is living a community life."

At the same time, by weaving this struggle into what it means to observe Ramadan, believers advance an understanding of religious agency in tune with the grammar of Islam. Contemporary understandings of urban religion originate predominantly from a Judeo-Christian perspective, which tends to focus on the private beliefs of individuals. This perspective contrasts sharply with a faith like Islam, in which the role of embodied practices comes to the foreground and into public view. Intending to please Allah in a morally treacherous environment is therefore part of the religious project that believers embark on — a project that intensifies during Ramadan as believers come together to fulfill their religious hopes and plans.

MAQ members were vulnerable to many of the negative neighborhood effects that have come to characterize life in a poor urban neighborhood. This vulnerability was evident whenever a believer asked for a ride, money for gasoline, or bus fare, as well as in believers' struggles to have enough food. For members like Elijah, the line between Ramadan and the rest of the year blurred, because they often limited themselves to one meal a day. Collectively, there was an institutional vulnerability in the masjid's ongoing struggles to pay its bills and maintain the property (which I examine in detail in chapter 2). These shared experiences informed believers' interpretations of Islam, and Islam informed how they navigated life in South Central, creating in turn a distinct type of lived religious experience in which individual hardship was woven into congregational life.

Living a Muslim community life in an environment like South Central means that piety exists *through*—not against—poverty. For this to make sense, we must disentangle agency from the tropes of resistance, coping, and adaptation in which social scientists have tended to frame the actions of people in poor urban neighborhoods. Doing so allows us to give credit to successes while remaining sensitive to the structural forces that hinder abilities to achieve intended goals. To see piety as deepening by engaging hardship also requires going beyond Western understandings of religion as a privatized system of individual beliefs to include notions of faith as embodied and necessarily public.

Islam informed believers' desire to make good intentions, but their lives as African Americans in South Central often shaped the specific content of these intentions. Making good intentions, then, represents a particular kind of agency, one exercised within a religious framework that strives for purposive action based on what is perceived as right. In this framing of believers' ideas, Islam provides an ethical code for believers to draw from in determining what actions to take. I found that during Ramadan, believers at MAQ did this by positioning their actions in relation to those of the non-Muslims around them, which stood in contrast to their inward-looking activities the rest of the year. Apart from Ramadan, they sought to please Allah by, for instance, earning money through halal economic activities. These activities may or may not be legal under US law; but by selling religiously sanctioned goods off the books, believers can situate their informal economic activities as morally superior to the haram markets around them—namely, the drug trade and sex work. I examine these activities in greater detail in chapter 3.

During Ramadan, believers' intentions heighten; but they also come up against the everyday hardships of life in a poor neighborhood, where there are more people in need than resources to go around. Food is one of life's most basic necessities, yet it's one that too often escapes the lens of the social scientist. Being forbidden to eat by one's faith has a way of drawing greater attention to what hunger means, both at an individual level and at the wider social level. At Masjid al-Quran, believers had to work out who should go hungry when food was scarce, though for those with more resources at home (or even a home to go to), the struggle was more symbolic than material. Still, even to a better-off believer like Naeem, the stakes were high, because the goal is to please Allah and avoid hellfire. However, the opening for a different form of agency available through religious participation at MAQ was limited. As we will see throughout the book, pious agency is structured by and within local social, political, and economic contexts. Believers at MAQ have creatively worked the immediate environment and its structural dimensions of urban disadvantage into their formulations of what it means to be Muslim. They intend to do right by Allah not despite the neighborhood but via direct engagement with it. Understanding how this tension is worked into a particular way of being Muslim at MAQ deepens what it means to be *believing in South Central.*

CHAPTER TWO

"Don't Move. Improve"

The evening started like many others that first Ramadan. I pulled my Honda Accord into the masjid lot just before sunset, ready to observe believers making *salat* (prayer). As I made my way to the communal area outside the prayer hall, however, Brother Naeem stopped me.

"Have you heard the news about Imam Mohammed?"

I shook my head and told him no. He then explained that Imam W. D. Mohammed, the revered seventy-four-year-old African American Muslim leader based in suburban Chicago, had "returned to Allah" (passed away). Mohammed, son of Nation of Islam leader Elijah Muhammad, was the most influential African American Muslim theologian in the country.[1] I expressed genuine surprise, saying I had listened to NPR most of the day and heard nothing about it. Naeem shrugged. "They were probably talking about Obama and McCain, right?" It was September 2008, and the presidential election was in full swing. Then he changed the subject, telling me about another masjid he had visited last night.

The call to prayer sounded a few minutes later, so we headed silently into the prayer hall. Once the sunset prayer Maghrib finished, Imam Khalid approached the microphone. He announced what everyone already seemed to know: Imam Mohammed passed this morning at his home near Chicago, although the cause was still unknown. "I talked to Elijah Muhammad Jr. today," Khalid explained. "The circumstance as known now is that Imam Mohammed was home alone where he was planning to be picked up to perform a *janaza* [burial]." According to Khalid, when the brothers went to pick him up, they found him unresponsive in his hot tub, which, Khalid quickly added, "he had for his health. . . . But he was not sick. He was not ill of any kind. He was sittin' in the Jacuzzi but did not drown."

Calmly, Imam Khalid urged the believers, "Remember what it says in the

Qur'an. He gives life and gives death." After a brief pause, he added, "Nothing stops because one of us passes away." Khalid said he would leave tomorrow for Chicago and planned to pass along any news to Brother Fareed in the masjid office. "Go eat your food and say a *dua* for Imam Mohammed," he urged.[2] Then, with a firmer voice, he declared, "We are still going to be our own man and own woman," assuring members that even if help is brought in, "our leadership is solid . . . whoever comes in is gonna be a part of the Elijah Muhammad past." He concluded by reminding believers, "Crying is okay, but grieving is not." Grief is a sign of not letting go. Since Allah controls who dies, we must accept His will and move on.

Back outside, I found Sister Haleema. She looked sad, but when I asked whether she was, she shook her head. "I'm not sad, I'm just . . ." She never finished her sentence. Instead, she called Brother Sulayman over to talk.

Sulayman, who had family back in Chicago, told Haleema that the janaza was planned for Thursday morning, but "some people are discussing."

"Discussin' what?" Haleema asked.

"Well, there's something over it," Sulayman replied.

"A cloud," Brother Ricky chimed in.

"Yeah, a cloud over it," Sulayman agreed. He added that Imam Mohammed's passing happened so suddenly that there were "questions," but not wanting to desecrate the body with an autopsy, "they'll" probably "forgo" trying to stop the janaza.

Haleema, who claimed to be the "first one local who heard" about the imam's passing, made an oblique reference to her son's death a few years ago, saying something about "not having a choice" with an autopsy.

Later, while I waited for dinner under the tent with Naeem, he asked me, "Will you include a chapter on Imam Mohammed?" I explained to him that it may not take up an entire chapter, but I would mention Mohammed and the leadership of the Nation of Islam. Nervous that he'd be offended by this, I was instead surprised by his response: "I think it would be more interesting to see the reactions [to the imam's death]." He explained that what "should" happen is the janaza taking place within three days, whereupon people would move on to the estate, which "should" be split between the wife and kids, as laid out in the Qur'an. Naeem guessed that some family members "will get emotional" and may fight such a settlement of the estate, but that wasn't what "should" happen.

*   *   *

The news of Imam Warith Deen Mohammed's passing brought twice as many believers to iftar than was typical for a Tuesday night—seventy instead of the usual thirty-five. Brothers wore long faces, and some sisters had tears in their eyes, including Sister Ava. Yet, following the directive of Imam Khalid, there was no sobbing, no shouting, no conspicuous grieving. The most visible sign of loss was the embracing among believers: men hugging, women hugging, men and women hugging each other. As they embraced, believers asked one another, "How did you hear about Imam's passing?" That question was followed by "Where were you?" It reminded me of how my parents spoke about the day of President John F. Kennedy's assassination and the years afterward, remembering "where you were" when you had heard the news and the patriotism fostered by the moment of collective effervescence from mourning the president's death. However, unlike Kennedy, for whom the nation came to a virtual standstill to mourn, the passing of Imam Mohammed came with little public fanfare. I doubt that most Americans would even recognize his name, even if they know a bit about his father, Elijah Muhammad.

But for members of Masjid al-Quran and the estimated hundreds of thousands of African American Muslims who followed his teachings, Imam Mohammed's death may be most comparable to the sense of loss and uncertainty Catholics feel when a pope dies. Of course, there is no pope in Islam, as Imam Khalid pointed out. Islam is a decentralized religion, with no international leader. This means that national and local leaders take on added significance.[3] In the case of African American Muslims, leadership includes national-level figures such as Imam W. D. Mohammed and his father before him, along with local mosque leaders like Imam Khalid. But the death of Imam Mohammed represented a major turning point for the tens of thousands of believers across the country who were his followers. By examining how members of MAQ reacted, we can better understand how and why they frame the past as an integral part of their contemporary interpretations of Islam. This history making remains important for the social organization of the community, including its emphasis on economic uplift and racial pride.

"I Know We Feel Like We're Rudderless"

Five days after Imam Mohammed's death, Imam Khalid was back in LA, and the community gathered for a special meeting. I recorded some of the proceedings in my field notes:

> Arriving just before noon, I count fifteen believers clustered inside the masjid, including part-time imam Louis Abdullah, Sister Haleema, Brother Fareed, his adult son, Fareed Jr., Brother Kareem, Brother Jarrel,

Brother Malcolm, Sister Natalie, and others. Sitting on the floor next to them, Imam Khalid opens: "Since our community was established in 1931 we have had a succession of the same leadership. It started with the Honorable Elijah Muhammad and continued with his son, Imam Warith Deen Mohammed. But it also ended with Imam Mohammed . . . I know we feel like we're rudderless and have nothing to focus on—[*a few yeses ripple through the audience*]—but we do what people focused on when Prophet Muhammad died." What people did during that time was move forward by living in accordance with the Prophet's practices (Sunnah), Khalid explains. Then he adds that Imam Mohammed "pointed us to [this] Islam." He turned temples into mosques and "decentralized" the organization, because he did not believe in one person as leader. "Now what has changed?" Khalid asks. His voice is soft, at times too low to compete with the sounds of the street. "Every change that happens is started by Allah. The Qur'an tells us Allah has plans, so His plan supersedes all else. Sometimes, even good things do not happen because Allah is not ready."

Over the next forty-five minutes, Khalid recounts the history of the community, starting with Elijah Muhammad's beginning and his efforts to grow the Nation in Detroit and later Chicago. He continues, "So Elijah Muhammad was in the tool kit of Allah. Imam Mohammed was too. He was our leader. The Honorable Elijah Muhammad started with nothing in Detroit by Master Fard. Allah had to approve of that." Then, as he would repeat often over the years, Imam Khalid recognized their shared history as members of the Nation, saying, "We never would have entered Islam another way!"

Let me pause for a moment and point out that Khalid opened this special meeting about Imam Mohammed by going back in time to the late leader's father, Elijah Muhammad. Khalid often did this when lecturing to believers, repeatedly referencing their shared history in the Nation of Islam to highlight how far they had come—spiritually, socially, and politically—as a community of African American Muslims. The year 1975 marked a major turning point for believers, because it was the year Elijah Muhammad died and his son, Warith Deen, turned followers toward a radically different way of thinking about Islam. Khalid called on this religious pride again on that September afternoon in 2008:

By now the crowd has grown to thirty, with Brother Naeem entering late and making *salat* before joining the group. Khalid keeps going: "No other Muslims knew our needs," he said, referring to Muslims in Africa, Asia, and Saudi Arabia. "[Elijah Muhammad] wanted us to learn Islam our own way first. . . . He wanted us to rule ourselves!" This prompted several shouts of "Yes!" from listening members, including "pioneers" who started out in the Nation and had helped establish the original MAQ community, like Natalie, Jamil, Fareed, Haleema, and more.[4]

Attempting to assuage fears about the possibility of an "outsider" taking over in the wake of Mohammed's passing, Imam Khalid declared, "We don't need to go outside our community to do this! We have grown enough we can do this ourselves. This is what Imam Mohammed said week before last." Khalid tries to convince the small crowd that the community isn't lost despite feeling rudderless. "Our leadership is indigenous Muslims and will remain indigenous."

Just when the meeting seemed to be reaching an end, Khalid's voice suddenly turned louder. Not muffled by competing noises now, he warns, "Shaytan [Satan] is always there. . . . You have to wade through the muddy waters." But, he adds, "We can protect each other." Then he calmly reminds believers that "Islam is a way of life," and this is "a balanced community." He adds, "We're still *his* community, we're stilling following that, we're still following the Qur'an."

I noted in my field journal that this was the most intimate interaction I had observed between Imam Khalid and believers. I could comfortably make the same claim ten years later. Often aloof, Khalid maintained both physical and social distance from the masses at MAQ. He preferred to eat iftar in his office, away from the communal tables where believers sat. He refused to discuss politics with anyone who did not vote, telling me, "I'll talk to them about religion," but they are "not qualified to talk about [politics]." And when he lectured or delivered announcements, he stood tall, letting his lankiness assume an almost magisterial quality over the adoring believers looking up at him. But on that day in 2008, sitting on the floor, his shoulders slightly deflated, Imam Khalid seemed more human—the captain of a rudderless ship drifting toward a distant horizon.

The Legacy of "the First"

As Imam Khalid alluded to in his special meeting, the Nation of Islam began in Detroit with "just a handful of people." That handful included W. D. Fard (pronounced *Fah-rahd*), "a mysterious peddler-turned-prophet," and Elijah Poole, "a Southern migrant with aspirations to religious preeminence."[5] Poole, who would later change what he called his "slave name" to one that matched Islam's holy Prophet, believed that Fard was a deity from Arabia sent to awaken Black people to their rightful religion. Fard recruited an estimated eight thousand followers in Detroit, including Poole, before moving to Chicago in 1933 to escape police harassment.[6] We know little about what happened in Chicago in the coming years, except that Muhammad (Poole) took over leadership of the organization around the same time that Fard disappeared, never to be seen or heard from after 1934.[7]

During the next several years, the group known by whites as a "Moorish cult" or "black voodoo cult" began to recruit more Black men and women from the streets of the South Side of Chicago. Muhammad's teachings asserted that the man whom he referred to as Master Fard "had been a divine manifestation, and that Muhammad himself was Fard's sole representative, the 'Messenger of Allah.'"[8] Muhammad claimed, "I know Allah, and I am with him," adding that "all blacks represent Allah . . . for all blacks are divine."[9] In representing God in embodied form, Muhammad sought to redefine Blackness as the "primogenitor of all that exists," and, in so doing, framed the Nation of Islam as a tool for teaching Black Americans to love themselves and to feel empowered to "do for self."[10] This latter phrase was one I heard repeatedly over my years of fieldwork.

Muhammad gained public notoriety with his controversial teachings and quickly drew the attention of multiple arms of law enforcement.[11] In May 1942, federal authorities arrested him for encouraging draft resistance, and he served four years in a federal correctional institution in Michigan. Rather than spell the end of the movement, Muhammad's time in prison allowed him time to teach. He began a prison ministry from his cell, teaching religion, philosophy, and Black history to fellow inmates. Prison ministry would prove critical to the movement's growth over the coming decades, and it remained important for recruiting new members under Imam Mohammed. Even today, two of the six imams who regularly led jumah services at MAQ worked as prison chaplains.

When Muhammad left prison in 1946 and returned to his position as head of the Nation of Islam, membership had dwindled to an estimated four hundred people, mostly men. Muhammad was a changed man, though, and soon after his release revised his theological messages to focus on economic uplift, moving away from the mysterious doctrines of the early years. He said, "We have to have businesses" and "You have to produce jobs for yourself."[12] He opened a restaurant and a grocery store, teaching his young children how to butcher meat and making entrepreneurship part of family life.

At this point, the Nation of Islam began to experience moderate growth, with a small but loyal following based in the Midwest and along the East Coast. Then, as Imam Khalid put it, "Malcolm came onto the scene." Born Malcolm Little, the street hustler converted to Islam while in a Massachusetts state prison. Upon his release in 1952, Little traveled to Chicago to find Elijah Muhammad and to ask what he could do to spread the faith. He traveled to Detroit, Philadelphia, and eventually to New York and back up through New England. It was at the Moorish Temple in Connecticut that Imam Khalid said his mother first saw the charismatic minister and decided that all thirteen of her children had to hear him. She "wouldn't rest until each of us had gone to temple once to hear Malcolm." While at first Khalid resisted, in 1955 he eventually went; what he heard "was so powerful," because it focused on actions, not just ideas. Khalid liked to say that the Nation of Islam was a religious *and* a social movement, in which members learned to see "hard work" as a practical tool to fight racism and poverty. The emphasis on action and cultivating practical tools for Black progress reverberated in Imam Khalid's teachings fifty years later, as when he said in 2010, "The best of us are those that are most useful."

Members of the Nation transformed themselves spiritually, socially, and physically, and adhered to a strict dress code that represented order and respect. Gone were the "zoot" suits popularized by African American musicians in the 1940s as well as other clothing associated with street hustlers.[13] Enter the single-breasted suits, skinny ties, and black-rimmed eyeglasses epitomized by Malcolm X. Brother Naeem joked that he first entered the temple in Los Angeles in the early 1970s dressed like a pimp. He later learned that such presentations of self were strictly banned. The Nation's internal police force, the Fruit of Islam (FOI), had "soldiers" who checked everyone before they entered the mosque to ensure that all men and women were properly dressed. MAQ literally had a "check room" where members underwent physical inspection before entering the masjid. One brother described the process as taking out the "rough edges" and smoothing members into respectable figures. Men were expected to wear clean, pressed suits; women had to display modesty by covering their heads, arms, and legs, their uniforms reminiscent of those worn by the Garveyite Black Cross Nurses.

Leaders in the Nation also encouraged marriage, a disciplined diet, and abstinence from alcohol and drugs, all of which Elijah Muhammad framed as tools for learning to love oneself and for defying white Americans' negative stereotypes of Black people. Racial pride became fused with religious asceticism, and believers learned that by practicing self-maintenance, they could better the Black community. In a self-published memoir, Brother Saddiq wrote of his time in "the First" (Nation of Islam), "I considered myself a man of G–d when I was F.O.I., and one of the main things I liked about Elijah Muhammad was that we were commanded to do righteous deeds in our community. It was my duty." This emphasis on duty allowed believers to feel they were taking control of a life too often deemed static and inevitable as Black Americans segregated into an urban "ghetto." Saddiq explained that men were required to "be fruitful and multiply, buy a house, eschew credit [*riba*], start a business, and protect and provide for a large family." He said that this directive worked. He fathered six children with a wife he considered his soulmate, achieving his own version of the American dream. "I got the money, good homes, and friendships in all walks of life that he [Elijah Muhammad] promised. Astonishingly, if you consider how small my world was at that time. As an F.O.I. my nation was within a five-mile radius of [MAQ's first address]." That Saddiq could accomplish what he set out to do within South Central was instrumental to his sense of religious selfhood and his masculinity.

Nation of Islam members were "rehabilitated and put to work" because, as Imam Khalid said, idleness was not allowed. Leaders enforced rules through an informal court system. Offenses could be minor, such as sleeping in the temple or chewing gum, as well as those perceived as more egregious, such as drug or alcohol use and adultery. If found guilty, members were "given time" in excommunication. "I don't remember anyone getting thirty days," Khalid said, adding that the exclusion from fellowship usually lasted a minimum of ninety days, giving members time to "learn to obey."

Adults expected the youth to also adhere to strict rules of self-discipline. Children attended the University of Islam, a Muslim parochial school located at their temple. Believers boasted that the university was the "largest Black education system" in the United States, with over one thousand students enrolled in NOI schools across the US. Like their parents, who were expected to line up in the check room before entering the temple, children lined up every morning to enter school. Saddiq, who worked as a teacher at one of the NOI schools in LA, recalled, "We had an assembly. . . . You came in late [*snaps fingers*], drop, give me ten, in your suit." He said the Nation focused on "results, not excuses" for *all* its members. The University of Islam schools taught Black youth in poor urban areas like South Central to love and respect an essentialized view of Blackness. Parents perceived the messages taught in the Nation schools as a "welcome change from the white-oriented teaching in nearly all public schools."[14] Curricula included courses on Nation of Islam theology and Black history, the latter not yet available at most US colleges or universities.

Elijah Muhammad and his ministers also transformed how followers earned money. The organization began selling newspapers in the early 1960s and by 1975 reached a circulation exceeding half a million. Imam Khalid remembered going door to door in his hometown of New Haven, Connecticut, to sell copies, saying the newspaper was the single most important way that the Nation spread its message to Black communities. Clearly, the Gramscian argument that elites use the media and other "ideological sectors" for control was not lost on Muhammad.[15] With great skill, he combined print media, religion, and education to engineer a different kind of consent of rule within urban communities, drawing heavily from his newspaper, *Muhammad Speaks*, to advocate economic separation from mainstream (white) America. The messages published in the newspaper created what Imam Khalid called an "effect," encouraging believers to join the movement and help it spread. Years later, when pushing the renamed *Muslim Journal*, Khalid pleaded, "[We] cannot let this paper die."

As important a role as the newspapers played in MAQ's organizational growth, what most Americans remember about the NOI during that period are the "corps of bow-tied men hawking bean pies."[16] Bean pies are custard pies made with white navy beans and whole-wheat flour, which Elijah Muhammad said were cleaner and healthier than the sweet potato pies popular in Southern soul food. Members of MAQ went into the streets of South Central to sell their pies, with many non-Muslim residents becoming regular customers. These interactions helped members gain the trust of their Black neighbors and family. Brother Naeem bragged to me, "If there are two things *this* community gave society, it's Islam . . . and bean pie." Pride in its past in the Nation of Islam helps explains why, more than thirty years after transitioning to Sunni Islam, the MAQ community, Imam Khalid included, continued to sell the *Muslim Journal* and homemade bean pies.

For MAQ's members, the focus of the Nation was never on hate but on "love of self," with this mantra offering an ideological alternative for poor, disenfranchised Black residents. Hard work, moral asceticism, and racial pride created a potent agentic mix that gave believers hope that a different future was possible. As Brother Louis, MAQ pioneer and part-time imam in the community, put it, "[Elijah Muhammad] had a plan to bring us to Islam, an awkward plan but it worked. It was Allah's plan. Under our own color, under our own leadership."

The Rise of a "Ghetto" Counterpublic

The Nation of Islam grew rapidly during the late 1950s and early 1960s as a result of the appeal of Elijah Muhammad's race empowerment ideology. In 1956, it had ten temples, concentrated in the Midwest and along the East Coast. By 1975, that number had increased to more than one hundred throughout the United States, including the one established in 1957 in South Central.[17] As with many NOI temples, MAQ members had little choice but to set up their community in one of the poorest and most blighted areas of their city. Until World War II, few Blacks in Los Angeles lived or worked outside South Central. Even after the Housing Act of 1949, these residents continued to live behind a visible color line, segregated into the dense area south and southwest of the downtown business district via restrictive covenants and redlining practices.

Forced residential racial segregation allowed city officials to essentially ignore the problems of Black Angelenos by keeping them physically contained in an undesirable part of the city. For much of the twentieth century, municipal funds earmarked for traffic safety, sewerage, street repairs, and so on were diverted from poor Black areas to wealthier white neighborhoods. City officials also "ignored or relaxed zoning ordinances to accommodate commercial growth in residential areas," enabling several chemical companies and food processing plants to set up in the area around the NOI temple.[18] The industrial debris and hazardous waste these plants produced turned South Central into the "dump-yard of the city of Los Angeles," driving down property values and creating public health crises.[19] Along with its physical deterioration, South Central offered residents fewer employment, transportation, and retail options.

Ironically, all this helped the NOI temple strengthen its foothold in South Central during the 1950s and 1960s, creating new jobs and retail options for Blacks trapped in a depressed urban environment. In his famed 1961 account of the Nation, sociologist C. Eric Lincoln wrote, "The Muslim leaders tend to live and to build their temples in the areas from which they draw their major support—the heart of the black ghetto. The ghetto houses the most dissident and disinherited, the people who wake up to society's kick in the teeth each morning and fall exhausted with a parting kick each night. These are the people who are ready for revolution."[20] The NOI reinterpreted the problems of the inner city—unemployment, municipal neglect, commercial divestment, poor housing—as opportunities for Black residents to reinvent themselves by becoming "soldiers" for the movement. Temple leaders walked through the streets of the neighborhood recruiting poor, disenfranchised residents. New recruits learned that the Black man would rise out of poverty through self-discipline, knowledge, and hard work, not by depending on government assistance or anything originating in white America. The Nation viewed politics "as an extension of righteous behavior, a tool with which to achieve the race's destiny."[21] Members didn't seek new laws to govern change but advocated instead for the principle of self-determination to govern the individual. This emphasis on economic separatism distinguished the Nation from other Black political movements of the 1960s. Under the leadership of local ministers, temple members in Los Angeles established fish and soul food restaurants, grocery stores, and bakeries. These brick and mortar operations, combined with the bow ties and bean pies, raised the profile of Muslims in Los Angeles. Said Imam Khalid, "We didn't eat pork and didn't sell it. We didn't smoke and we didn't sell cigarettes. We didn't sell alcohol. They said you couldn't survive in business if you didn't sell those things. We showed [them] wrong!"

Not everyone could be so easily convinced to see the positive influences that the Nation produced. Many powerful and wealthy whites in the city perceived MAQ members as "aggressive" and "militant."[22] Within a few years of its founding, the community found itself in several physical confrontations with law enforcement. In 1961, members of the old NOI temple clashed with white security guards outside a grocery store on Western Avenue. According to Los Angeles historian Josh Sides, "Six Muslims (five of them under the age of twenty-five) attacked the guards, stomping and beating them."[23] The event contributed to perceptions that the Nation of Islam promoted violence, despite members' persistent claims that weapons weren't allowed, and violence permitted only in self-defense.

Over the next several years, the situation with law enforcement worsened. LAPD engaged in a "campaign of repression" against the NOI temple and its members, including surveillance and organized violence.[24] The campaign reached its climax in 1962 in what believers described as a "fierce run-in" with the police. Officers raided the temple, supposedly in search of weapons. Community members said the officers "shot up the masjid" without just cause, killing one brother, paralyzing another, and injuring five more. The police never found any weapons on the men or in the building, and by all published accounts it was indeed an unprovoked attack. A jury of twelve whites would later rule the shooting justifiable in the trial that followed.[25]

The shooting outside the Los Angeles temple became a turning point in the history of the Nation of Islam. Malcolm X had helped establish and build that community, and he was close to the murdered brother. He perceived the LAPD raid as a personal attack on his religious beliefs. At the funeral for the slain brother, Malcolm told the audience of more than two thousand mourners,

They were praying when they were shot down. They were saying, "Allahu Akbar." And it shook the officers up, cuz they haven't heard Black people talk any kind of talk but what they [whites] taught. And two of the brothers who were shot in the back were telling me as they lay on the sidewalk they were holding hands. They held hands with each other, saying, "Allahu Akbar," and the blood was seeping out of them where the bullets had torn into their sides and they still said, "Allahu Akbar."[26]

After the funeral, Malcolm pressured NOI headquarters to fight back with physical force against the police in Los Angeles. Eljiah Muhammad rejected the notion, advocating instead for patience and encouraging Malcolm to channel his energies into economic activities. The two men's divergent views on how to pursue justice contributed to Malcolm's later retreat from the Nation and, more generally, indicated a growing ideological schism within the organization, signaling that "two different visions of religious identity" were forming within the movement.[27]

While Nation leaders quarreled in Chicago, back on the ground in Los Angeles members of the local temple thought "the war was coming" with LAPD.[28] Imam Khalid said that it was the success of the Los Angeles brothers in "reaching hearts and minds" of people in the Black community that threatened police, not actual physical force. He emphasized that officers found no weapons the two other times they "broke in" at the mosque in the 1960s. The Nation didn't teach violence, Khalid emphasized, pointing out that members lived in the neighborhood and for the most part "prevented violence."

Few scholars writing about race in Los Angeles have devoted attention to this moment in the city's history, in part because the police department and the whites that dominated it successfully framed the Nation of Islam as a militant group rather than a religious movement and consequently minimized the shooting in public accounts. Instead, the arrest of Marquette Frye by a California Highway Patrol officer in August 1965 became the watershed moment when racial injustice manifested in social unrest, culminating in six days of rioting in and around the Watts neighborhood. It was the deadliest and most expensive of the more than one hundred urban riots that spread across US cities in the 1960s.[29] Yet even if the city had forgotten about the 1962 shooting of an unarmed African American Muslim man, believers at MAQ had not. The event remained significant enough in the collective memory of members that forty-six years later, they shared the story when I first entered the masjid, recounting the loss of the brother and pointing to this past violence by LAPD as proof that African American Muslims have always faced discrimination from law enforcement. This was their response to questions I asked about 9/11 and whether the terrorist attack brought additional police attention to the MAQ community.

Despite violence and intimidation, members of the African American Muslim community in Los Angeles continued to build their economic empire. Sisters cooked food, made uniforms, and taught children, while brothers sold newspapers and ran businesses; none of the proprietors were over the age of thirty-five. When Imam Khalid took control of the temple in 1973, he added a dry-cleaning business and led the community's successful fish importing operation. The Nation imported thousands of pounds of whiting fish every week from Peru, which brothers received at the Port of Los Angeles and transferred to the community's warehouse in South Central. These transactions brought African American Muslims into contact with foreign entities, a far cry from the perception of the inner-city "ghetto" as isolated and disconnected.

In fact, the MAQ community was experiencing so much growth—financial and otherwise—that members needed more physical space to hold meetings and to educate children. The Los Angeles chapter of the Nation of Islam purchased a nearby building, and in one weekend members transformed a music venue into a religious and educational facility. Khalid boasted that they didn't wait for city permits before making the changes, although such defiance would later prove costly after a protracted dispute with the City of Los Angeles over the use of a commercial property for schooling.

Believers perceived their actions in the early 1970s as building Black solidarity and contributing to economic uplift in South Central. They organized bazaars, plays, conferences, festivals, and other events, often inviting non-Muslim African Americans from across the city to participate. The events drew famous Black entertainment and sports celebrities as well as local politicians, including the city's first African American mayor, Tom Bradley. In Imam Khalid's recollections, these events weren't so much about teaching religion as they were about building history, culture, and business. He said the intent was to create a sense of "belonging" and "togetherness" built on racial pride.

The "Transition"

By the start of 1975, the Nation of Islam was experiencing "unprecedented prosperity."[30] Under the control of Elijah Muhammad and his "royal family" based in Chicago, the Nation owned a bank, a publishing facility, an airplane, refrigerated trucks, an extensive import business, orchards, dairies, thousands of acres of farmland, apartment complexes, and hundreds of small businesses, like the those in South Central.[31] This was in addition to the more than one hundred physical temples across the country. Altogether, the Nation amassed an empire worth between $80 million and $110 million. Imam Khalid said that it took scientists forty years to build a rocket to go to the moon, but only forty years for Muhammad—a man whose family was "born into slavery"—to build a community worth $100 million. It helped the Nation become, as C. Eric Lincoln noted, "the most potent organized economic force in the black community."[32]

So it was nothing short of astonishing for believers to watch all this disappear over the next few years, following the death of Elijah Muhammad on February 25, 1975. Plagued by lifelong respiratory problems, the seventy-seven-year-old had died of congestive heart failure the day before he was supposed to address twenty thousand followers in Chicago for the annual Saviours' Day celebration. These loyal women and men instead received the news of Muhammad's passing and learned that his son, then known as Wallace Deen Muhammad, would succeed as leader. "The Nation of Islam was at a crossroads," Lincoln noted in the postscript to his famed account of the movement.[33]

Wallace Deen took the stage that February day and announced the beginning of a series of dramatic changes to the organization of the Nation of Islam and to its theological foundation. He explained that W. D. Fard was not God in flesh but a "manifestation" of God to Elijah Muhammad.[34] He argued that "being black did not mean that one was a god or even a member of the chosen race; being black meant having the 'black mind,' which was a symbol for closeness to God."[35] He told followers they needed only the Qur'an now to achieve salvation. Imam Khalid was among those in attendance for the Saviours' Day celebration, later becoming one of the seven original ministers who stood on the stage and declared his allegiance to Wallace Deen. Choking back tears, Khalid recounted, "On that first day, fifteen thousand ears opened to Islam."[36]

Like Khalid, many believers pointed to 1975 as the year of their (second) new beginning, both in their personal relationships with Allah and in their understanding of religious community. Rejecting the term *conversion*, believers instead called this their "transition." Many adopted new Arabic surnames, replacing X with names such as Muhammad, Hasan, and Abdullah. Over the next several years, W. D. Muhammad, who changed his name to Warith Deen Mohammed to further distance himself from his father's legacy, encouraged African American Muslims to look toward Islam as a "way of life" where racism has no place. He also implemented several changes at the local operational level, turning temples into masjids and ministers into imams. He ordered the removal of all chairs so that believers would, in Khalid's words, "learn salat as Muslims around the world do." These alterations to the style of ritual changed the rhythm and tempo of community life by reorganizing the mosque to be open for five daily prayers and jumah on Fridays. Believers, who previously fasted at Christmastime, now began to fast during the holy month of Ramadan and in so doing joined more than 1 billion Muslims who follow a lunar calendar for religious holidays. The University of Islam schools became Sister Clara Muhammad schools, keeping a connection to Elijah Muhammad but drawing new attention to the importance of women in the community. And, perhaps most controversially for members of a Black nationalist movement, Mohammed opened masjid doors to non-African American people. He did this, Khalid said, "at the expense of losing some of the hard-shell people."

Imam Mohammed then moved toward opening believers to a new world in which they saw themselves as members of a global religious tradition.[37] He encouraged interethnic dialogue between "indigenous" and "immigrant" Muslims. Conditioned to follow orders under the leadership of Mohammed's father, members at MAQ pursued the changes with dedicated zeal. Just one year after hosting a Black Business Bazaar, they organized a bazaar that included immigrant Muslims, shifting the event's focus from "buying Black" to "supporting Muslim businesses." A video of the event featured an Arab teenager receiving a scholarship, a symbolic gesture of the community's new efforts toward greater racial inclusion.

Imam Mohammed struggled with how to nudge the members of the Nation of Islam toward a race-inclusive ideology while at the same time recognizing their unique experiences as Black. Some believers resisted this change, especially when the imam insisted on opening the masjid to whites. Brother Jamil said, "We lost a few people. Some people were still hanging on to their old beliefs and ways." Though Imam Khalid portrayed the community's transition as taking place overnight (and perhaps personally it did), Jamil admitted that it took closer to "a year and a half" for most of the members to transition.

Some scholars have suggested that the "mainstreaming project" of Imam W. D. Mohammed would have failed without the concomitant rise in social positioning that many members experienced, thanks both to the movement's Puritan-like asceticism and to the general progress of the African American community at large during the 1970s.[38] However, as a large portion of the movement underwent this "subtle class shift," a rift began to develop between those members who were experiencing modest upward mobility and those who remained poor.[39] The schism widened in the next year, when the Nation of Islam faced economic collapse.

Elijah Muhammad's death exposed that the organization was deeply in debt, owing many creditors for mortgages and loans it couldn't pay. Imam Khalid said, "We were told to sell businesses, and we did." The money went to the people running businesses, leaving some members better off than others and creating tensions that would intensify in later years. But it was the organizational side that proved most consequential. "We did make one big mistake," Khalid admitted. "We didn't close out the temple as a corporation." When leaders transferred the businesses to individuals, MAQ was left with a "staggering" tax bill and faced a two-hundred-thousand-dollar lien on the property. "In the end, everything we worked so hard for [was] deemed personal," Khalid said. After taxes, whatever was left went to attorney fees.

While Imam Mohammed may have been an excellent spiritual leader to believers, it's clear he made critical missteps in the legal process of disaggregating the Nation's business holdings. The losses were staggering for MAQ, but not wanting to focus on the negative, Khalid said that that was "the nature of these things." It seems likely that not everyone at MAQ took this sanguine a view about the community's losses, but no one publicly blamed Imam Mohammed. Instead, they spoke longingly of their days in the Nation, often referring to pioneers by what they sold (e.g., Brother Nathaniel who "used to have the bakery"). In this way, loss became reframed as part of believers' identities and proof of their shared survival.

There Goes "the 'Hood"

As members debated how best to deal with the demise of the community's financial stability over the next several years, the neighborhood around the masjid changed in ways that made past strategies of recruitment and fundraising less tenable. Believers might have been able to rebuild their businesses using the entrepreneurial acumen they had cultivated in the Nation were the local consumer markets in South Central able to privilege African American cultural tastes, but the social-spatial regime was changing, just as MAQ was turning from a temple into a mosque. Whereas the neighborhood was majority Black or African American when the community purchased its new building in 1973, by 1990 that population had dropped to 30 percent. The area became increasingly Latino in ethnic composition, with immigrants from Central America taking over the homes of former Black residents. A similar demographic shift occurred throughout the County of Los Angeles (see table 1). The Latino population increased from 1,288,716 (18.3 percent) in 1970 to 3,359,526 (38 percent) in 1990.[40] Whereas the number of Blacks increased by 175,730 in the same period, their proportion of the city population declined from 10.7 percent to 10.46 percent.[41] This may not seem like much, but in certain areas of the city the changes were much more dramatic. Between 1970 and 1990, the African American population decreased from over 80 percent to less than 20 percent in MAQ's neighborhood.[42] By 2010, less than 10 percent of residents living around the mosque identified as Black or African American.

The demographic transformation of South Central greatly altered the urban experience for MAQ members.[43] Gone were the fish fry and soul food restaurants they once frequented or in some cases owned. The streets around the mosque became home to *pupuserias*, *carnicerias*, and *pana-*

TABLE 1. *African American and Latino Populations of Los Angeles County, 1950–2016*

Year	African Americans	Percentage of total population	Latinos	Percentage of total population
1950	214,897	5	249,173	5.7
1960	459,806	7.5	582,309	9.6
1970	755,719	10.7	1,288,716	18.3
1980	924,774	12.3	2,071,530	27.5
1990	931,449	10.46	3,359,526	38
2000	930,957	9.5	4,242,213	45
2010	934,619	9.6	4,599,258	47.1
2016	940,943	9.4	4,861,648	48.3

derias. The influx of Latino immigrants and the cultural transformation they initiated in the area—what historian Josh Sides terms the "Latin Americanization" of South Central—likely prevented the area around the masjid from becoming the vacant wasteland that parts of the South Side of Chicago became in the 1980s, but it also created new obstacles for believers to find jobs or secure housing, particularly as Spanish became the more dominant language spoken in shops and restaurants.[44]

At the same time, large companies that once provided decent jobs with benefits for low-wage workers, including Goodyear and General Motors, relocated their manufacturing facilities from central Los Angeles to areas too far to be reached without an automobile. With few public and private transportation options, residents couldn't get to jobs in outer-ring areas.[45] A growing number of residents (including many believers) struggled to make ends meet in the constricted local labor market and found themselves increasingly dependent on government assistance to support their families.[46]

Finally, compounding these instabilities was the emergence of the crack-cocaine trade in South Central in the early 1980s and the related rise of gang violence in the area, which helped spawn close to two decades of historically high homicide rates.[47] The MAQ community felt the threat of violence firsthand when it lost yet another brother in the early 1990s, this time from a stray bullet during a gunfight between warring gangs. The man was painting the fence around the masjid when he was shot. Members planted a bush sunflower in his honor, where it remained in 2008.

Some members responded to the rise in violence and loss of jobs by moving out of Los Angeles and relocating to surrounding counties, as did many other African Americans.[48] A few continued to attend MAQ for religious services and special events, commuting as far as ninety miles *each way*, but their attendance was understandably sporadic. Those who moved to wealthier neighborhoods on the western edge of South Central joined newer mosques in the commercial corridors of Crenshaw and Leimert Park. MAQ faced the challenge of sustaining its Muslim, historically Black community in a religious ecology that increasingly favored Latino Christian denominations.[49]

Members who remained struggled to make sense of the newly unfamiliar neighborhood, which no longer looked or felt like *their* South Central. Directing her gaze to her house down the street, Sister Rasheedah recounted that once the "Hispanics moved in," she stopped leaving her door unlocked the way she did when the area was "all Black."[50] Later in this same conversation, she blamed former Black neighbors for introducing her then teenage daughter to crack cocaine in the 1980s. In trying to reconcile these contradictory experiences, she said at another time that she has "some Mexican American" neighbors who look out for her, but she lamented that it "isn't the same."[51]

Whether the influx of Central Americans to South Central in the 1980s and 1990s led to an actual increase in crime is less important here than the perception that the neighborhood was no longer as welcoming to African American residents. We might think of this as the shrinking of an imagined community, where the number of people with whom members felt they could identify grew smaller. Ironically, the sense that the neighborhood was inhospitable probably helped the mosque hang on to members who, like Sister Rasheedah, found themselves spending more time there to be around people with whom they identified.

Then in April of 1992, almost to the day thirty years earlier that a Muslim brother died at the hands of LAPD, the MAQ community watched as the streets around it burned in the costliest civil uprising in US history. The 1992 riots/unrest that began in South Central and spread to pockets throughout the city ignited after the acquittal of four police officers who had been caught on tape violently beating African American motorist Rodney King in March 1991. When the unrest was over, at least fifty-two people were dead, more than two thousand were injured, and the city faced over $1 billion in property damage, with many buildings in South Central burned to the ground. Brother Fareed said he stood at the fence of the masjid watching cars go by, their passengers throwing bricks at nearby businesses before jumping out to "take stuff." I asked how the masjid fared, and he said, "They saw us but didn't bother." Fareed attributed his safety and that of the masjid's to their fabled history in the Nation of Islam, because many residents feared the mysterious but strong "Black Muslims" who patrolled the streets.

However, it may be that there was no reason to attack the masjid, because what had once been a block of Muslim-owned buildings was by this point a nearly vacant acre lot of dirt and trailers with little to take. The once grand three-story building the community so proudly purchased in 1973 and hustled to pay off had suffered serious structural damage from earthquakes in the 1980s. The city declared the building unsafe and ordered that the community undertake large-scale (and expensive) repair. The loss of MAQ's commercial enterprises just ten years earlier combined with the shrinking size (and pocketbooks) of its members made retrofitting untenable. Believers had no choice but to tear down their beloved brick building, leaving a gaping physical hole.

MAQ stood at a crossroads: sell the land to "get out of the ghetto," as one staff member framed it, or attempt to rebuild on what was now a sizable plot of empty land in the middle of an urban field of gangs and industrial waste. Members decided to stay, believing it a wiser investment. Said Imam Khalid, "Our motto was, 'Don't move. Improve.'" Leaders rallied members to pitch in where their individual skills were needed by hammering, painting, installing electricity, and laying carpet to construct what was supposed to be a temporary prayer hall fashioned from a former school trailer. Leaders framed the teamwork as evidence of the community's ability to overcome any disadvantage. But the prayer hall would turn out to be a minor obstacle after what developed next.

"We Were the Laughingstock of the City"

With the immediate problem of where to hold services resolved, MAQ leaders began the arduous task of trying to raise funds for a new mosque. They secured promises from an overseas group of Muslim investors to help build a new structure, and as part of the agreed architectural plans, they mobilized to have a major excavation made for a subterranean parking garage. As the construction was taking place, the investors started to put pressure on Khalid and the organization to change its theological approach. The outsiders wanted MAQ to follow a stricter, more fundamentalist doctrine. Khalid refused. He wanted MAQ to maintain its religious autonomy and to stay rooted in its African American legacy, including its history in the Nation of Islam. The investors backed out. The community was left with a massive hole and no money. The hole later filled with rainwater and became known, quite disparagingly, as Lake Qur'an. In the words of Imam Khalid, "We were the laughingstock of the city."

MAQ had to wait years before an immigrant Muslim from another mosque donated the dirt and trucks needed to fill the hole. In the process, the community spent thousands of dollars in permit fees: first for zoning approval from the city to begin excavation for the garage and later for permission to refill the hole with dirt after the project was, according to official city documents, "abandoned." These expenses would be significant for any small organization but proved especially cumbersome for a community that collected only $600–$1,200 per week in contributions from members.

With the "lake" behind them, leaders at the mosque turned once again to Imam Mohammed for advice on where to start rebuilding. He recommended that MAQ build a school, emphasizing that education is of utmost importance in Islam and key to the future of the African American community at large. Khalid called on members to give for what was supposed to be a private Islamic school. He also sought donations from other Muslim communities, both in the United States and overseas. The plans were drawn up in 1999 and the school completed in 2006. Soon before it opened, however, the community realized there were too few members to finance a private parochial school, so they were forced to lease the building as a public charter school. It opened with a student population that was 22 percent African American, the other 78 percent being Latino. By 2011, those percentages were 16 and 83, respectively. Although Imam Khalid's wife worked at the school and several of the board members came from the MAQ community, many believers felt they had lost the school to the now Latino neighborhood.

Almost ten years after the school opened, the community had yet to initiate phase 2 of the architectural plans, which included a new mosque and recreation center. Leaders were struggling for the means to finance it, with believers feeling tapped out. No one expressed disappointment with the advice Imam Mohammed had given to build a school before a masjid. Several believers had choice words for Imam Khalid, with some accusing him of malfeasance; but toward Imam Mohammed they professed undying support, because it was under his guidance that they had "found" Sunni Islam. At a 2009 memorial for the late leader, Khalid said, "What [Mohammed] did in the twentieth century will be with us in the twenty-first, twenty-second, and twenty-third centuries . . . for our children." And that is why the moment of Imam W. D. Mohammed's death felt like a turning point, one in which members were unsure of where the tide would take them.

A Leader Lost and a Community Still in Transition

Following Brother Naeem's advice on that September night in 2008, I studied MAQ members' reactions to the death of Imam W. D. Mohammed. Contrary to Brother Sulayman's estimation that the imam would be buried immediately in accordance with Muslim tradition, the Cook County medical examiner performed an autopsy on the seventy-four-year-old man. The results surprised me. The examiner's report suggested that Mohammed had died of a possible heart attack *days before* being discovered. If we accept Imam Khalid's account, it was then that a group of Muslim brothers found the body—not Mohammed's fourth wife or one of his many children or grandchildren who lived in the Chicago area. It seemed a sad ending for a man described by the *New York Times* as the "Top U.S. Imam" and a man revered by millions of Muslims around the world.

Yet importantly, I didn't learn this melancholy news at MAQ, instead reading about it in obituaries in the *Chicago Tribune, New York Times,* and *Los Angeles Times.* Not once did I hear a believer or leader mention the autopsy or reports of Mohammed's body lying undiscovered for several days (except Ava, whom I prompted), and I observed and participated in thousands of conversations. I find it unlikely that members did not know. Brother Fareed was a voracious reader, never without a copy of some newspaper on his desk in the main masjid office. Imam Khalid was considered part of Mohammed's inner network, as was Sister Haleema. And many more believers had direct connections to the Chicago African American Muslim community, including Sister Aisha, whose husband served on the security team that traveled with Imam Mohammed. I think believers preferred to remember the leader in his glory days, just as they approached "community" and "neighborhood" as ideal types. Nostalgic about their activities in the Nation of Islam and the days when South Central was "all Black," they actively drew from positive accounts of the past and ignored its blemishes.[52] And who could blame them? With a past defined in many ways by struggle and loss, perhaps ignoring the fact that the man who led them to Islam died alone is an act of community survival.

* * *

Though we call something history when it happened decades earlier, remembrances of the past are integral to contemporary lived religious experiences. Believers at MAQ went through the rise and steep fall of the Nation of Islam, entering a new version of Islam in the mid-1970s with great uncertainty. The decades since their transition to Islam have been marked by repeated loss—the loss of the brick and mortar businesses that helped the Nation gain its foothold in South Central, the loss of their beloved physical masjid, the loss of Black neighbors, and the loss of safety on nearby streets. Yet believers remain committed to their faith and the promise that their community may one day rise again to serve as a force for good in the neighborhood. It's partly their nostalgia for past glories that gets members of this aging religious community to show up every Friday, climbing the rickety stairs of the masjid dressed to the nines. Their clothes can sometimes reflect a different era—wide-lapel suits, wingtip shoes, and fedoras with the tint of time at their edges. One sister, Natalie, even continued to wear the thick polyester homemade women's uniforms of the Nation. Believers saw and experienced all of it, making this "history" an integral part of their contemporary experience. Even the leadership of the community is still there: Imam Khalid has gone from a man hand-selected by Elijah Muhammad to lead the Los Angeles temple to today's captain of a rudderless ship.

I once asked Brother Fareed, Khalid's right-hand man and masjid treasurer, "What's the biggest issue facing the community?" He replied, "What you said: building a community." He went on to say that we're all just people, and no one is better than anyone else. "You aren't better than me, I'm not better than you." But to get to the point where members could understand their worth, Fareed said that African American Muslims needed W. D. Fard and Elijah Muhammad. "A lot of people think the Nation taught hate," he continued, "[but] the Nation did not teach hate. It taught self-love."

Believers understood that the challenges ahead of them were substantial, but they also drew from their shared past as evidence of an ability to survive against the odds. Masjid al-Quran may have been a place of tattered majesty, but the former temple that triggered Malcolm X to leave the Nation has withstood urban riots, police violence, and economic failure. It could have been a very different history had the community not been able to maintain control of its property after the transition from the Nation to Sunni Islam in 1975; but in their perseverance, believers maintain a commitment to their shared belief that African Americans are, in Khalid's words, "a beautiful but strange people" who do best when managing their own communities. Only by putting into social context the ways that believers have embarked on a pattern of striving and struggling for the past fifty years can we appreciate what it meant for Imam Khalid to tell believers that the loss of their esteemed leader, Imam Mohammed, would not spell the end of the community's sovereignty as African American Muslims. And only then can we reassign agency to their practice of a race-conscious form of Islam that has taught them to love themselves, their community, and their neighborhood.

CHAPTER THREE

"Money Is Funny"

The Marketplace

Brother Sharif stands outside the prayer hall with a large plastic cooler at his feet. As the believers file out of jumah, some stop and peek inside. A sister asks Sharif what he has this week. He bends with stiff knees and lifts the cooler lid, pointing to plastic bags of frozen lamb and chicken sausages. The sister hands Sharif several dollar bills and walks away with a bag of halal meat.

Six feet away, Brother Fareed slumps into a metal chair under a portable tent. On the table in front of him is a wicker basket with a typed sign reading Zakat ("tax" on wealth). Inside the basket are several dollar bills and a few bills with Lincoln's face. A brother stops by the table.

"As-salaam alaikum, Fareed. How you been, Brother?"

"I can't complain," Fareed replies. Every now and then, someone drops a ten or a twenty into the basket or hands Fareed a check. If requested, he produces a carbon copy receipt with Tax-Deductible stamped on it.

Just then, Sister Ava turns her rusted car into the gravel lot, kicking up dust. She scrambles out of the driver's seat and around to one of the rear doors, pulling out a large black plastic milk crate. She yells to Brother Elijah to get the other crate. When he doesn't reply, she shouts louder: "Elijah!" He turns and sees Ava point to the car. Elijah ambles over, leaving his van and his merchandise in the corner of the lot. He grabs the other crate and carries it to where Ava has set up, next to Sharif. She's already collecting money from the waiting customers and handing out clear plastic containers holding generous square slices of frosted cake. Ava tells her customers the price for a slice is now three bucks instead of two, blaming rising food costs. Some of the men around her grumble, but one brother smiles and asks whether she takes Visa, Mastercard, or the "We Be Broke card." "No, baby," she replies starkly. "Just cash."

Sister Aisha walks over and reaches inside the crates, pulling out several slices. Ava doesn't snap at her or slap the woman's hand like she does with children or some of the brothers. Instead, when Aisha picks up a slice of lemon cake, Ava asks, "That for Bat Mama? How she doin'?" Aisha explains that her family had to put a padlock on their gate because her mother-in-law, suffering from dementia, "got out" again, dressed up in her Sunday best and ready to go to church. Then she promises to go to the ATM down the street to get some cash for the cakes.

In the paved part of the mosque parking lot, Brother Jamil has set up a long table to display several books, their covers faded and their edges curling. The books have titles like *Elementary Teachings of Islam* and *The Prescribed Prayer Made Simple*. Also on Jamil's table are several T-shirts featuring Arabic phrases or African imagery, all in size XL or XXL and costing fifteen dollars each. When a group of believers make their way to his booth, Jamil lifts a briefcase from underneath the table and places it on top, opening it to reveal several "Islamic watches," as he calls them, with attributes of Allah inscribed in Arabic on their faces. Meanwhile, Brother Shaheed is walking the property, carrying a cardboard box holding copies of the most recent issue of the *Muslim Journal*. Several believers stop him, paying $1.75 for the Illinois-based weekly newspaper affiliated with the late Imam W. D. Mohammed's association of African American–led mosques.

Someone taps my arm, and I turn to see little Ali holding two small boxes of soap in his hands, one labeled Inspired by Paris Hilton and the other Inspired by Chanel. I ask how much. He tells me $3.50 each. He's helping his dad out today and is dressed for business, wearing a light-grey pinstripe suit with the brand tags still on the sleeves. I thank Ali but tell him I'm going to pass. He slumps down in a chair, looking bored. Sister Haleema marches up. "What are you doing, boy? Get selling! Get to selling! Make sure you give your dad that money!"

Elijah has returned to his metal clothing racks and cluttered table of used children's shoes, toys, and small kitchen appliances next to his rust-colored van. He's humming a blues tune as he folds shirts. A Mexican woman who rents the house next door has her stuff set up on the sidewalk corner just outside the gate. Together, their merchandise generates the attention of a few people on the street, but unlike the woman, Elijah can't communicate with potential customers in Spanish. I ask him whether people are buying today. He smiles and draws out his words: "Money is funny." After a long pause he adds, "They lookin' but ain't buying. Their money is funny."

A typical Friday at Masjid al-Quran included any one or all of these economic activities. "Vendors," like those in the above composite from my field notes, set up portable tables and tents outside the prayer hall. From these "booths" they sold a variety of goods to their Muslim "customers," transforming the masjid into a temporary halal marketplace. Determining what was permissible to buy and sell, as well as when and how, occurred within an Islamic moral framework. No one sold *haram* (forbidden) items like pork or alcohol, and during Ramadan vendors stopped selling food and drink. In fact, little market activity went on at the mosque during the fasting month. As a result, Fridays were much calmer during the fast, with the religious holiday Eid al-Fitr signaling both the end of the month-long fasting and the mosque's being open for business once again. Goods consisted mostly of food and drink, clothing, toiletries, jewelry, essential oils, new and used books, newspapers, and audio recordings of *khutbahs* (sermons)—recordings that until 2010 came on cassette tape. Many of the items had a subtle religious quality: Sharif's chicken sausages as an alternative to the pork ones sold in local stores; Ava's gelatin-free desserts. Other products were more overtly religious, such as books illustrating how to pray and an assortment of head coverings (kufis for men and fashion scarves for women).[1] Some items fused religious and racial meanings, like T-shirts printed with African symbols or the small bean pies that originated in the Nation of Islam. Believers also offered one another services, like a shoeshine or haircut; others handed out business cards or flyers for their car repair and travel services.

Economic activity helped structure social relations, with participation in the mosque market a key way of sorting out who was a full member at MAQ as opposed to just a visitor.[2] The sale and consumption of goods were so ubiquitous that believers became identified by what they sold. There was the "Cookie Guy" who resold cookies and pies from a local Muslim-owned bakery; Ava the "Cake Lady"; "Brother Malik with the juices"; and "Sister Sara with the purses," who took over for her husband, Jamil, after his unexpected death in 2009. Sometimes, believers forgot the actual name of their fellow Muslim brother or sister and instead identified members only by the product(s) they sold. On one memorable Friday afternoon, Imam Khalid stood at the microphone after prayer to announce details of an upcoming janaza. He said the brother's name, "Brother Abdul Muhammad," with several believers murmuring, "Who?" Imam Khalid added, "The brother with the cookies every week." Only then were there nods of recognition.

Though they were small in monetary value—a few dollars here and there, maybe up to forty for a purse—exchanges were significant in two primary ways. First, it was clear that some believers needed to sell in the mosque market to make ends meet. Many had been cut out of the formal labor market decades ago; others never really entered it. Both sets of employment histories fit within a larger story about the lack of paid work in South Central, where unemployment rates in some parts soared to 40 percent in the 1980s, the period in life when many believers would have been at their highest earning potential.[3] Ava liked to say, half-joking, half-exhausted, "The only jobs in LA, the ones you gotta make up." Like Brother Sharif, she pushed through the pains of an aging body engaging in physically intensive labor because retirement was a luxury she couldn't afford. In this way, every dollar exchanged at MAQ counted toward someone's overall well-being, whether earning or spending.

That said, it would be wrong to suggest that participation in the mosque market was motivated entirely by money. Exchanges were small in dollar amount but carried rich moral currency, making them significant in a second, more culturally specific way. Participation in halal commerce was part and parcel of the shared moral project believers engaged in as a blueprint for social change. It was one of the ways that they demonstrated good intention outside Ramadan and, like other modes of religious action at MAQ, integrated into living a Muslim way of life in South Central. "We want to compete on a material *and* spiritual level." That's what Khalid's protégé, Imam Ahmad, told believers one Friday, capturing the community's discontent with its economic positioning. Gazing toward a better future, believers strove to improve their economic lives through Islamically appropriate modes of action — framed to be in direct opposition to what others in the neighborhood did to make ends meet. Striving to earn money at the mosque deepened religious commitment, an extension of mixing economics and theology that had begun for believers in the Nation of Islam and constituted a form of religious community building. It was why children as young as nine learned to participate in the market and why Ava could count on Aisha to buy cakes every week.

But Imam Ahmad's words capture another important element of economic activity at MAQ: competition. Resources were limited and the circuit of commerce closed off from larger revenue streams. In this chapter, I show how leaders promoted entrepreneurship and Muslim commerce as part of one's piety at MAQ and how believers, in their attempts to compete on a spiritual level, ended up competing with one another in ways that strained the bonds of religious community. Money is indeed funny when there's too little of it and the struggle to survive is unrelenting.

"Muslims Are People of Action"

"In the old scripture, we were told that idleness is devil's workshop [*sic*]. And you can look at people who are idle, who don't do anything productive, and you can see in their life the devil is working, Shaytan is working on them." Khalid's voice starts rising. "Look at the idle people who just stand on corners. What are they doing? They're talking nothing and either half-drunk . . . they either smoking something that is bad for their health or drinking something that is bad for their health, and speaking something that is very foolish. They are not productive people. Muslims are not like that!" Several believers shout "Yes!' "Uh-huh!" and *"Takbir!"* Khalid continues, "Muslims are people of action—not inaction, but action! We get married! We take care of our wives! We take care of our children! We take care of the house, of the family!"⁴

It wasn't uncommon for believers to doze off when Imam Khalid taught, even though his khutbahs rarely lasted longer than thirty-five minutes. The prayer hall was often stuffy, and the imam's voice frequently got drowned out by the sounds of the street. But on this otherwise unassuming February afternoon, he generated several shouts from the audience as he reinforced a dichotomous way of thinking in which idle people on nearby corners ("they") aren't productive like Muslims ("us"). Believers' affirmations echoed the call-and-response style of worship common in many Black churches in which participation from the congregation heightens the emotional intensity of worship.⁵ Believers became animated like this when called on by a religious leader to resist stereotypes that lump residents of South Central together as an amorphous population.

Though the economic transactions at MAQ were off the books in that most cash or in-kind exchanges occurred without receipts or formal record keeping, believers clearly didn't see their activities as part of a larger informal urban economy in South Central.⁶ Rather, they took great pains to position their economic practices as morally distinct by putting their halal trade in direct opposition to other ways of making ends meet. This boundary work—built on a long history of respectability politics—furthered a shared sense of righteousness among members, strengthening their identification as a religious community. For example, Ava's catering work was meaningful beyond just her earnings, because it demonstrated her fortitude in resisting the quick wealth that can come from illicit activity. She liked to tell people that she refused to talk with her sons when they were in prison for dealing and that she had rejected the gifts or cash they tried to give her from their drug profits. To prove to herself and others the morality of her off-the-books business, Ava said she had turned down offers from some family members to put weed in her cakes. She claimed that this addition would have earned her four hundred to one thousand dollars per sheet cake, up to twenty-five times what she charged for a regular cake. Instead, she said she chose to "hustle" in an ethical fashion, spending Fridays selling at the mosque and the rest of the week selling to employees at local businesses as well as vetted referrals from family or close friends. She perceived her halal hustles as making her a better Muslim who was more moral than the people she knew who were "slangin'" (selling drugs) or "hookin'" (engaging in prostitution).

Attendant to this way of understanding commerce is the implication that one may not earn much from such economic efforts, but it's the intent that matters to Allah. "Whatever we've done in the past, we can do better," Imam Khalid taught. "We can always do better. There's A-plus and A-minus, so if you got a B you can do better. If you run a mom and pop store, you can do better, get more patronage. If it's a Muslim business, bring a flyer to the office, because we need to develop culture, saluting people who believe." With a rising voice, Khalid continued, "Expect more out of self, get more. Do good as Allah has done good to you. Can anyone say Allah has not been good? So, you don't have money? You made it to jumah! You are here." Working hard constituted part of being a *good* Muslim. This explains why Elijah sometimes spent eight hours selling at the mosque without "making a dime" but still found pride in his efforts.

Running a Muslim business was an important way of distinguishing oneself as an ethical subject, an act made more meaningful for believers who wanted to distance themselves from activities in their past. Take Brother TJ, whom I met in 2008 as he was approaching three years out from an eight-year term in prison. With quickened speech punctuated by shoulder sways and hand jabs, TJ told me he was originally sentenced to "twenty-five to life" but spent his time inside learning about the law. Now living in an SRO near downtown, TJ said he was volunteering with an organization on Skid Row that helped inmates receive legal advice. He was also working to develop a travel website, which he proudly showed me on the laptop he carried around the masjid. He also had at his side a small duffel bag stuffed with hats, hair accessories, and other items for sale. Sounding sincere about his business ventures, TJ chanted that a man's "gotta do, gotta do," emphasizing his intention to be a person of action.

As Tatiana Thieme has argued, hustling can be both aspirational and survivalist, allowing people "on *their own terms* to face conditions beyond their control."[7] In her study of young waste workers in Nairobi who collect garbage from their neighbors for a fee and then either dispose of or resell the waste, Thieme found people combining "the urgency of everyday economic survival with aspirational urban identities" so they could make their everyday struggles more meaningful.[8] A similar process occurs at MAQ with the fusion of religion and moneymaking. Believers create "a form of pragmatic politics" through their informal economic activities at the mosque that allows them to respond to unjust conditions in the neighborhood.[9] The official poverty rate around MAQ hasn't dipped much in the fifty years that it's been in its present location. When the mosque opened its doors, 30 percent of the neighborhood's residents lived in poverty, and today the rate is closer to 40 percent (where it has hovered for decades). Nor does there appear to be much relief in sight. Since the 1992 riots/unrest, poverty rates have increased in three out of the four main quadrants in greater South Central.[10] Turning an informal economy "into a form of pragmatic religious politics allows believers at MAQ to reclaim some of the power they have lost as a result of their exclusion from formal labor markets.

"Do for Self"

The many links that believers and leaders drew between piety and work reveal just how strong the legacy of the Nation of Islam continued to be in contemporary MAQ community life despite the community having transitioned to Sunni Islam decades earlier. Economic self-sufficiency was a cornerstone of the Nation, with founder Elijah Muhammad teaching followers that the blueprint for Black economic success rested on one's ability to *do for self*.[11] Followers accepted that they had to work hard, be frugal, and avoid debt, and they believed that doing so would free them of the self-hatred caused by centuries of racism. Furthermore, by frequenting Black-owned businesses, especially Muslim-owned ones, and practicing clean living, believers heard from Muhammad that they could "enjoy salvation in the here and now."[12] Fast-forward five decades and leaders at MAQ were still stressing economic self-sufficiency and hard work as keys to salvation, although now in less race-specific language.

Also at the time of Muhammad, leaders in the Nation of Islam emphasized that the key to Black liberation was through *shared* economic progress. Muhammad instructed members to "pool resources," "recognize the necessity for unity and group operation," and "give employment to your own kind."[13] It was a form of Muslim liberation theology that took a traditional Protestant ethic of individualism and situated it within a longer history of Black struggle.[14] In *Message to the Blackman in America* (1965), Muhammad wrote that Islam would help Black Americans "think in terms of self and their own kind" and that "this kind of thinking produces an industrious people who are self-independent." He was attempting to reorganize followers to envision themselves as autonomous subjects able to create their own destiny, to change the conditions of Black people in America through their own efforts rather than relying on whites.[15] "Do for self" became a rallying cry for members of MAQ, with the belief that economic self-sufficiency attained through pious means is part of achieving a righteous community. In a community that has been systematically stripped of economic opportunities, "do for self" returns a sense of agency, especially when coupled with piety. If a believer hustles but does not achieve his or her intended gains, there is still the good intention to prove oneself a pious person to keep that individual part of a larger moral project.

In continuing to run and support Muslim businesses to this day, believers have also learned to see their actions as a form of social support. Under the contemporary constellation of "do for self," believers help one another by making their individual hardships part of a shared struggle to lift up fellow Muslims. It represents a form of care work that tries to alleviate religious kin's financial pain and suffering. "Care," write Annemarie Mol and colleagues, "seeks to lighten what is heavy, and even if it fails it keeps on trying."[16] We see this care in how Aisha bought cakes from Ava every week and how she helped Ava cook when there was a catering order too big for one person to handle. Aisha didn't think she could alleviate all of Ava's financial woes; it was more about helping Ava carve out her own path to economic survival. With this economic activity, the mosque became more than a space for worship; it was transformed into a hub for a particular form of commerce in which piety was distinctly social. Like a cooperative, which aggregates the market power of people who on their own could not achieve as much, the moral economy at MAQ generated positive ties while seeking to empower believers.[17] In other words, even when economic uplift fails to materialize to desired ends, it's the practice of intending well toward others by supporting their business that matters to Allah. This, too, becomes a way of being a *good* Muslim.

However, in coming together to create a system of halal exchange, it wasn't always clear how to balance individual needs with those of others. As a customer, you likely see your purchase as helping a fellow Muslim sister or brother, but with limited personal funds you also need to watch every dollar. So maybe you make a joke about being broke so you can get a better price. Maybe the vendor sees through the joke this time and tells you, "No, baby." But in another instance, she knows you've had some recent family struggles and tries to do what she thinks is right for a fellow Muslim by offering a deal. She can't have everyone find out, or they, too, will point to their hardships for a better price, undercutting her business. So the vendor offers the deal in secret. You and she feel satisfied, thinking you've both been good Muslims. Then maybe someone finds out about this deal and gossips about it, casting a shadow over the vendor. It's a small community, and word gets around quickly that this vendor is not to be trusted, because she gives some people better deals than others.

Now imagine that the vendor is the mosque. The scenario just became much more problematic, especially since most members would benefit from financial help. Believers reframed the "do for self" ideology of the Nation as a contemporary cultural blueprint for how to be pious amid disadvantage, but it was a blueprint requiring many shades of gray. And that shadiness could undermine the good intentions of believers and leaders. As sociologist Kai Erikson argued in his classic study of a coal-mining town in Appalachia, culture is rarely as unified as people want to believe.[18] Instead, we are better off conceptualizing culture as "a kind of theatre" where people play out different ways to think, act, feel, and imagine.[19] Sometimes, imaginings in this moral space will be contrary to one another, and it's precisely in charting the points and counterpoints of the theatre that we can better understand the messiness of economic culture at MAQ.

"You Think Just Because They're Muslims They Won't Steal"

Sister Hafsa and I were sitting in traffic one Friday night, on our way to an off-site masjid fund-raiser, when suddenly she realized she no longer had the plastic bag containing her after-jumah purchases. She began frantically searching around the passenger seat, repeating, "I can't believe I did that. I can't believe I did that."

"Why can't you just get it tomorrow?" I asked.

"Because," Hafsa said, "it will be gone. People always take your stuff there."

I reached behind my driver's seat and into my purse to grab my phone. I pulled up Ava's number and handed Hafsa the phone. "See if Ava's still at the masjid." In a panicked voice, Hafsa asked Ava to look for "a plain bag, you know, like from the store," with "two pies and some avocados." I could tell from listening in that Ava had found the bag. Hafsa asked her to hide it where no one could find it. Ava did one better—she promised to take it home and return it to Hafsa tomorrow. Then Hafsa ended the call and settled back in her seat, relaxed.

When she calmed, I took the opportunity to ask Hafsa more questions. "If someone at the masjid finds the bag, with only the bean pies and avocados, won't they keep it for a day or so, in case a fellow believer comes back for it?"

Hafsa didn't answer my question directly but instead told me two stories. The first involved a sister who misplaced her scarf inside the masjid prayer hall. When she told another sister about it, the second woman pulled a scarf out of her bag and said, "Like this?" She apparently thought it had been left out for taking. In the second instance, the "Cookie Guy" had his stock of cookies stolen when he went inside to pray. Hafsa concluded, "You think just because they're Muslims they won't steal."

My conversation with Hafsa highlights two important points about economic activity at Masjid al-Quran: first, the intensity of her reaction to the possible loss of two mini pies and a handful of avocados revealed just how precious even small amounts of money were to some members, especially older ones on fixed incomes. Second, her comment that people at the masjid will "take your stuff" felt like a warning: don't assume you can trust your religious brothers and sisters.

I began to see other markers of trust issues within the community that heightened my awareness of the suspicions believers had about one another's motives. Women always carried their handbags with them, or they went without. Every time Sister Dina, the imam's wife, prayed, she handed me her thick set of keys, unwilling to leave access to her car, apartment, and office unguarded for the five minutes of *salat* (prayer). When I started fieldwork, there were locks on the kitchen cabinets. Later, after a remodel replaced the cabinets with open metal shelves, a lock was placed on the door leading to the kitchen. The increased security measures at the mosque continued. In 2013, I noticed that the simple wooden padlocked donation boxes inside the masjid had been replaced with thick steel safes; their thin slots were for receiving checks and currency.

At first, knowing the high crime rates in the neighborhood, I assumed people in the community were responding to concerns about the potential for outsiders to enter the grounds and take things. It was one of the reasons the mosque made sure there was always on-site security. But as time wore on and I became privy to more backstage conversations between believers, I suspected that their fears stemmed also, if not more so, from distrust of fellow worshippers. Hafsa may have acted discreetly, refusing to provide names, but others were less delicate, and rumors swirled about who was "not to be trusted." Gossip thus served as a key way of learning whom to trust. Brother Malik, for example, was someone to buy juice from but otherwise best to avoid.

I also saw believers cultivate ambiguity about their available means in their interactions with each other. It went beyond jokes asking whether a vendor took the "We Be Broke card" and included elaborate stories to obscure any amount of wealth. Brother Naeem, for one, boisterously declared himself a "hood rat" and often described himself as broke—on one occasion saying loudly in front of a large group, "I couldn't get more poor!" But Naeem was a college-educated high school administrator, employed full time at a public school south of the city. His behavior seemed preposterous given how well known he was to other long-term members. Why would he say he was poor when he wasn't?

I believe that Naeem felt constrained. He rented an apartment in a part of the city known for its low-cost housing (a place called the Jungle), and he appeared to have limited assets. I also knew he had many demands for support from kin, including two ex-wives.[20] However, compared to many if not most members, Naeem was well-off. I came to see his public declarations as a deliberate strategy to minimize his chance of becoming a mark.[21] It suggested that Naeem expected a certain degree of exploitation, just as Hafsa expected to have her belongings taken if left unattended.

I took cues from believers and learned to be vague in conversations about money. I even went so far as to bend the truth on several occasions to prevent appearing moneyed, such as when I went on vacation and stayed in a nice hotel, or when I moved to the neighborhood and believers bluntly asked how much I paid for rent. The first time I told the true amount (four hundred dollars), I was told that I was paying too much. I learned to say, "a few hundred bucks." At the same time, as a white woman affiliated with an elite university, I was clearly privileged. And even those who didn't know about my education saw me as more likely to have money. At my first Ramadan, for example, a man I'd seen a few times but did not know approached me and said, "Sister Pamela, read this when you get a chance." He handed me a small torn piece of paper, which I read later during dinner. It asked, "Can you help me?" and requested eighty dollars, which he needed until the VA paid him in twenty-seven days. I found the amount unusually high compared with the amounts I typically heard people ask for at the mosque; a dollar or five here and there was more common, enough for bus fare or a light meal. I asked around about the man but found out little. Sister Haleema advised, "Uh-uh. I wouldn't. But Allah forgive me." When the man came up to me later that night, I told him, "I'm sorry, brother. I can't help you out. I don't have anything tonight." He looked at me with disgust, turning away and avoiding me the rest of the evening.

Returning to my notes from the previous night, I found that I had had a brief conversation with the man, who I noted as walking with a limp and having yellowed eyes. He told me he was going to the VA hospital for surgery that week and patted his stomach. Trying to be polite, I said the community would be thinking about him, but I later noted that no one else talked with him. Instead, people went out of their way to avoid him. Brother Naeem refused to shake hands when the man offered his. I don't know how the man knew my name, but I suspect he asked someone about me or listened in on my conversations. My niceness combined with my privilege made me a mark, while Naeem's coldness must have served as a cue to leave him alone. I never saw the man again, at the masjid or anywhere in the neighborhood.

"I Don't Trust No One Who Says They Don't Like Money"

Over coming months, requests for my help grew more elaborate. Rather than ask me directly for money, though, believers tried to draw me into "business opportunities." During my first year of fieldwork, I was approached on three different occasions with an opportunity by men within the MAQ community who wanted me to help them secure grant money to create a nonprofit (the assumption being that as a graduate student, I'd be an expert on proposal writing). I was told that in exchange, I could "make a killing" by taking a percentage of the grant. The men generally approached me when I was walking alone to my car, away from other believers. In one instance, the brother—a long-standing community member—handed me a handwritten note in all caps: "THIS LETERR IS FROM YOUR FRIEND RICKY OF MASJID AL-QURAN. AS-SALAAM-ALIKUM. SO WHATS UP PAM, REMEMBER LAST TIME WE TALKED I REMINDED YOU I MAY NEED YOUR HELP. WELL NOW IS THE TIME." The letter then explained Ricky's need for help locating statistics on the lack of jobs in the area and, as he put it, "data on how it effects a cummunity . . . Articles. Professors. ? Help." As I had done once before, I offered help in the form of unpaid research assistance, explaining that I was forbidden to make money on my research "per UCLA rules" (my simplified explanation for Institutional Review Board policies). Months later, when I followed up with Ricky, he was still struggling to get his nonprofit going. When I asked whether he was doing any of this to help the masjid, he said no. "I don't want no haters gettin' in it."

Because they approached me when I was alone, I worried that the men had other, less business-oriented motives, but Ricky's confession that he didn't want "haters" from the masjid getting involved suggested the secrecy was more about the community than me. Still, the combination of mistrust I had learned from believers and my unease about the ethical dimensions of getting involved in business ventures with people I was studying prompted me to avoid invitations like this one.

My lackluster approach to entrepreneurship meant that over time, no one else tried to start a business with me. It was a strategy that backfired, at least for a while. More than a few believers joked that as a sociologist, I "liked" poverty. On one such occasion, I joked back that I didn't have money because I didn't like it, to which Brother Fareed curtly replied, "I don't trust no one who says they don't like money." My failing to take on the role of "grant girl" (if I imagine a possible nickname) made me suspect to some, and my privilege in being able to avoid starting a business indicated I had other means. After that first year, I transitioned from a potential business partner to primarily a customer. I helped Ava sell cakes, but everyone knew it was because we were close and I had nothing financial to gain from running the booth.

"Don't Sign Anything"

Had it been only those employed in formal labor market jobs who drew requests for money, I might have written off the equivocation as a strategy of wealthier members. After all, who hasn't told solicitors outside the grocery store that they have no spare change? But even members known to have limited financial assets went to great lengths to appear less moneyed.[22] When Ava bought a van from Sister Aisha, she asked her friend to tell people that it was a gift. She didn't want anyone in mosque administration to know she had eight hundred dollars to buy the vehicle. She guessed that if Fareed found out, he would "hit [her] up" for money. Ava seemed almost paranoid about the men in the office and warned me early in my fieldwork, "Don't sign anything Fareed gives you." She didn't elaborate on why Fareed couldn't be trusted, feeling it was inappropriate to talk badly about a Muslim behind his back; but after I spent several years in the community, she told me that he had served time in federal prison for fraud. I located the case online and confirmed the charges.

Learning about Fareed's criminal history put an interesting spin on a conversation I had with him in my first year of fieldwork, when he tried to show me how even I, an educated skeptic, could be conned. He slipped into character mode and acted out the following plan.

Fareed swaggers up to me and brushes my arm with his hand. "Hey there, young lady. It's your lucky day. I just found this envelope with forty thousand dollars. You seem like a real nice person, so I tell you what, I'll split it with you." Then he pauses for dramatic effect. "See, I said it was your lucky day." Standing as tall as his short stature will allow, he continues, "I'm going to ask you to hold this, and then I'll come back and get it, okay? Hey, what's your name and address?" Then he pretends to write on the imaginary envelope he's holding. "Oh, by the way . . . you got a bank account? You do? Alright, then, let me take that down . . ."

I smile. "You've worked this out." Fareed just laughs. I'm incredulous and push: "There's no way people fall for that con. That's ridiculous."

"Oh, they do," he assures me. "They want some of that fast money." Then he adds, "Let me tell you something: the banks like that. They know about the forgery and they like it. They in it too."

We continue to debate the merits of his hypothetical scam a bit longer. Fareed explains that it was earning a living through "just talk," throwing it back to me. "That's what you do. That's what sociologists do. They talk for a living."

"Yeah, but our talk isn't illegal," I retort. Fareed just laughs and shakes his head.

I had playfully defended my profession as moral by referencing the law, but in doing so revealed that I did not (yet) get Fareed's larger point that legality is an imperfect gauge of right and wrong. After the charade, he told me that he never really worked in the formal labor market. "I worked once for a year. That was in 1955." Later he noted, "Ain't no one got rich carrying a lunch pail." I asked him what he did afterward to make a living, to which he replied, "You don't want to know."

Though Fareed claimed more than once that his old ways were in the past, believers joked about the seventy-four-year-old's trustworthiness behind his back. When the nephew of a long-standing community member stopped by the masjid one afternoon to visit with members, he saw Fareed walking across the property and said, mockingly, "Fareed still trustworthy?" Everyone burst into laughter. Ava, who was standing in the group, replied, "Oh, yeah, when Fareed comes around everyone be like [*puts her hands tightly over her pockets to cover them up*]." Jokes like this underscored how odd it seemed to have a man once convicted of bank fraud employed as masjid treasurer. Why would Imam Khalid let Fareed oversee MAQ's finances?

In fact, it makes perfect sense to have someone with a flexible moral code regarding money control the masjid coffers. Let me explain by returning to Ava and Fareed. Ava didn't trust her Muslim brother; that was quite clear. On more than one occasion, I watched as she handed him a ten-dollar bill for her week's zakat and, when asked by the treasurer whether she needed a receipt, replied that whatever he did with that money he would have to answer to Allah. The insinuation elicited only a rough chuckle or an exasperated "Psh!" each time. Yet Ava also relied on Fareed. She went to him for help when she couldn't pay her bills or needed a few bucks to hold her over until her next SSI check. He gave her small amounts of masjid money here and there, which Ava took with the understanding it was zakat for a Muslim in need. She was grateful, too, when Fareed turned a blind eye to how she sometimes "borrowed" food from the masjid kitchen. However—and here was the key problem—Fareed was secretive about his help. In private, he'd give Ava five dollars when she couldn't pay her bills and then in public charge her one dollar for using the masjid phone to call directory assistance. Experiencing Fareed's Janus-faced generosity fed Ava's conspiracies about the masjid and its treasurer, hence her warning me not to sign anything. It also caused her to hide her limited savings. Of course, by being vague and appearing in need, she also stood a greater chance of appealing to Fareed's charitable side.

"Where Does It All Go?"

The masjid had little in the way of public record about donations. Unlike churches, synagogues, and other mosques, where major donors are often acknowledged by name in congregational bulletins and email blasts, at MAQ people within the community who gave significant sums to the mosque often preferred that others not know exactly what they'd given. In five years, I only twice heard Imam Khalid acknowledge specific dollar amounts of key contributions. The omissions suggested that believers were more concerned with cultivating uncertainty about their economic status than receiving accolades or creating a paper trail to hold the administrative office accountable.

Given the masjid's need to be flexible with accounting, the lack of public records made sense. However, it created palpable tension between leaders and believers whenever money was discussed—which, given the community's needs and the emphasis at MAQ on moneymaking, was quite often. Consider this pitch for donations in 2009:

After jumah, Imam Khalid returns to the microphone. He makes the usual announcements about upcoming events, and then he updates the audience on his efforts to get a building permit from the city for MAQ's construction of a charter school. "We spent three hours downtown today, and they still haven't given us a permit . . . and, we still need that fire hydrant." He adds, "When I first told you about it last year, the cost was $16,374. But it's gone up $5,000 this year!" Several loud sighs fill the prayer hall. Some of the believers, exasperated, have already left. Khalid tells the remaining audience, "This is what they're charging us. We couldn't get around it. If you wanna wake up and come down at 7:30 a.m. with us [to the city offices], you are welcome. Just bring enough quarters. Bring enough for four hours. At $1 an hour that'll be $4."

Khalid's pitch had an outwardly antagonistic tone, challenging believers to go downtown and find out for themselves what was happening with the city. He concluded, "We've got the paperwork in the office, you're welcome to look it over!"

That day, the request for funds and the tone in which it was delivered were too much for several believers, including Sister Ava. It's always something, she complained. First the school, then this or that. "Where does it all go?" she demanded. We were standing in the kitchen just a few feet away from the staff office. She complained that the office didn't post expenses or collections, as was done at her friend's mosque. When we started talking, she was using a hushed tone, but by the end her voice was raised and defiant, calling the men in the office "shady." Then she teased me, playing off a long-standing joke about my fieldwork: "If you *are* FBI, go back and tell them!"

Not long after this conversation, staff began posting balance sheets in the office for believers to see the incoming and outgoing dollar amounts. When I asked Ava about it weeks later, she said, "That don't mean nothin.'" In her eyes, Fareed would never be able to shake his shady past, and his association with Imam Khalid made everything the two men did suspect.

∗ ∗ ∗

Requests for money from the organization, and subsequent spikes of exasperation among believers, took place throughout my fieldwork. Most often, these requests were for the "building fund" for a new masjid to replace the one torn down twenty years earlier. The organization, like the believers, had to hustle to make up for past losses. This communitywide hardship was woven into the social experience at Masjid al-Quran, much like the constant struggle to make ends meet motivated interpersonal interactions.

Were it just that the masjid leaders asked frequently for money, maybe their actions wouldn't have generated such frustration and outright animosity from members. After all, every religious organization in the United States needs donations from its members to survive, and believers knew it.[23] But what Khalid asked for at the end of nearly every jumah *felt* high to members—more than $21,000 for a fire hydrant one week, $2,600 for two window air-conditioning units another week. This in a community where members spent $100 to feed thirty-five people during Ramadan and where few members could afford the $65 ticket to attend the annual fund-raising banquet.

The figure that Imam Khalid quoted for a mandatory fire hydrant seemed high to me. By this point, I was deep enough into my fieldwork at MAQ to have acquired a heavy dose of skepticism toward anything involving monetary requests. So I called the City of Los Angeles and spoke with a planning supervisor. He told me that the school was responsible for paying to install a fire hydrant and that the average cost for one was around fifteen thousand dollars, with the cost increasing according to its distance from a main water source. He confirmed that an amount of $21,000 was reasonable for the area. I hung up, feeling guilty for doubting the veracity of Imam Khalid's claim.

Then came requests for money to pay rising property taxes. This struck

me as odd. Most religious organizations operate as nonprofits; their desig-
nation of a 501(c)3 status reduces or altogether erases many tax obligations.
I investigated MAQ's tax filings and learned that it had lost its tax-exempt
status. Not knowing what to do with this knowledge but determined not
to taint the data, I kept the information to myself. I waited to see whether
anyone else would question the need to pay property taxes. It took three
years, but in 2012 someone made his suspicions public. What happened
next threatened to undo the social bonds among several key members. The
scandal might have altered the future of the community if not for MAQ's
long history and deep commitment to staying rooted in its collective past.

*   *   *

Brother Asaad grew up in the community and graduated from the former
Clara Muhammad School. Named for his father, a pioneer who helped
establish the original MAQ community, the forty-year-old enjoyed the social privileges of a man whose family was revered as pious and hardwork-
ing. So when this well-respected brother and eldest son of Sister Aisha
called for the community's attention on something of utmost concern to
the masjid, believers listened.

Asaad said he discovered that MAQ had lost its eligibility for tax exemp-
tion under section 501(c)3 of the Internal Revenue Code after failing to file
the proper renewal paperwork three years in a row. His detective work also
revealed that Imam Khalid was head of a separate nonprofit organization
that held the deed to the public charter school property next door that had
been built with community funds. This was news to many believers. According to Brother Asaad (and supported by my notes), the rental income
paid to the masjid by the school had thus far never appeared on any masjid balance sheets. It wasn't clear how long Asaad had this information before going public, but once he did his actions were swift and dramatic. He
circulated a petition that called for the removal of masjid administration,
which Sister Ava was the second member to sign. She said she still loved
Imam Khalid, but this was business. Plus Asaad was the eldest child of her
best friend and a man she treated like a son.

Asaad's accusations against Khalid were substantial enough to generate concern among members. He held weekly community meetings to discuss his findings about the masjid's finances—meetings that revealed why
money was funny when mixed with religion at MAQ. The meetings started
the same way each week: Asaad would open with the latest information acquired from his sleuthing to a decent-sized audience (not as big as jumah
services but larger than a weekday iftar dinner). But within minutes, things
turned chaotic at all the sessions I observed. Members shouted at Asaad

and each other. Khalid's supporters saw the younger man as attempting a coup of their longtime beloved elder leader, accusing Asaad of wanting the masjid's money for himself. Asaad's supporters, meanwhile, were tired of the suspicion that seemed to blanket the mosque. Battle lines were drawn during these tense moments. One brother threatened to physically harm Asaad, while one of Asaad's supporters shouted that Fareed should not be treasurer, because he had been arrested for scamming people. Fareed was not present at the meeting, and in accordance with community interpretations of Islamic law, he had to be able to defend himself against any accusations for the discussion to continue. This probably explains why Fareed would leave the premises before the community meetings began—a tactic that Imam Khalid used as well.

The drama continued for several months, making for a tense year at MAQ. It seemed that every time I went to the mosque, I had someone whispering in my ear about a new person not to trust—Sister Ava warned me to be careful of what I said around Sister Aisha, whose other son was married to Imam Khalid's stepdaughter. Sister Dina warned me repeatedly not to share with Ava any of the confidential financial information I had access to as a result of volunteer work I did as a board member of the charter school next door to the mosque. I wrote in my field notes in 2012 that distrust was spreading like a disease. I started to think about wrapping up fieldwork, because the emotional toll of being caught between warring factions was too exhausting with a newborn (I had just become a mother). I continued to visit but scaled back my participation and resigned from my volunteer post at the school.

At first, Brother Asaad seemed unfazed by the drama. He organized a committee to rewrite the masjid bylaws in the vain hope that he would be able to rally believers to vote out the current administration. But he underestimated how strong the loyalty among his elders was, their need for constancy in leadership after decades of loss more important than financial transparency. Asaad's committee tried to operate as formally as possible, holding conference calls and taking official minutes. It didn't take long for that group to turn inward, though. Members accused Asaad of holding secret meetings with people outside the committee and using the committee to further a personal mission to become head imam. Six months after the original petition, Asaad was publicly kicked off the committee. He stopped attending MAQ except for limited special events, and took his growing bean pie business elsewhere. The rest of the committee continued to meet, but without Asaad, momentum fizzled. A set of revised bylaws was sent for approval to Imam Khalid, where it sat indefinitely. The topic then just seemed to disappear from conversation. All efforts to address alleged corruption in the administration faded, but the distrust continued and eventually spilled into the community marketplace, affecting relations among individual believers.

"Like Crabs in a Barrel"

Sister Lisa was one of the first believers to work with Asaad to raise the alarm and demand greater transparency about MAQ's finances. She was close with Asaad's mother and her daughters were good friends with his sisters. When Lisa joined the Bylaws Committee, she signaled her allegiance (and, by default, her distrust of Imam Khalid).

Lisa also ran a booth on Fridays selling boxed lunches and baked goods. She had started her business selling individual-sized sweet potato pies and brownies, and over time expanded the menu to include soup, fried fish dinners, cookies, and additional types of pies. Her booth took on the nickname "Café Lisa," complete with portable bistro tables and folding chairs. One sister joked that Lisa was running a Starbucks at the masjid, tapping into a common feeling among believers that the coffee chain charged too much for something you could get at McDonald's or 7-Eleven. As the café grew and took more time to set up, believers commented—out of Lisa's earshot—that she didn't always go inside to pray. Their implication was that Lisa was a little *too* ambitious in her "do for self" activities and that running a Muslim business should not come at the expense of spiritual development.

Within weeks of Asaad's public removal, Lisa began to sell her own version of his bean pies. It was a sign of betrayal to some believers, including Asaad's mother, who until that point had described herself as Lisa's "biggest customer," spending twenty to forty dollars per week on food for her children and grandchildren. Then Lisa started selling homemade "lemon dream pies," a knockoff of the gelatin-free lemon meringue pies that Sister Ava famously sold. Ava said Lisa was "biting off" her, complaining that it was "like crabs in a barrel" down at MAQ: as soon as one person started to climb up, the others in the barrel tried to grab hold to follow, only to end up pulling everyone back down. More believers started to complain about the café, emphasizing Lisa was too focused on making money. Meanwhile, Lisa continued to antagonize masjid administration. She distributed a flyer that accused Imam Khalid of not fulfilling his promise to complete the bylaws in time and "with concerns about integrity and internal committee tensions" announced that Sister Lisa resigned as chair of the Bylaws Committee. But the final straw came during Ramadan the following summer, when Lisa organized a separate Eid al-Fitr festival at a local park, collecting *sadaqa* funds that previously went to the masjid. Shortly afterward, rumors swirled that she had been "kicked off the lot" and was no longer allowed to run her café. Importantly, no one seemed sad to see Lisa go, not even her biggest customers. She had violated understood (if unspoken) rules about how far believers could take their Muslim business, and she lost friends as a result. With no booth left to operate, she reduced her participation in the community and sponsored only one iftar that Ramadan rather than the three or four she had in previous years. By 2014, Lisa and her family no longer attended MAQ, taking their business and zakat to another African American–led masjid.

With Lisa gone, Ava began to sell dinners and cakes again but in a more muted fashion. She was tired of all the "backbiting" and singled out Imam Khalid as a primary source of frustration. "I'm so ashamed of him," she confided. Ava wanted the imam to retire to allow the community to heal and move forward. Yet for all his faults, she added, Khalid was really a "good man," emphasizing that she loved him. Her ambivalence about him must be understood as part of the working out of what economic self-sufficiency looks like in a community where nearly everyone, even the organization, struggles.

From everything that happened in 2012 and 2013, it seemed as though community life at MAQ had become almost entirely about money. Even leaders aimed to "do for self," sometimes at the expense of the common good. On the other hand, if were it all about money, then believers likely would have kicked out Khalid or Fareed. The fact that they wanted to keep the administration the same, ignoring some suspicious behaviors, suggests that members were unwilling to lose more.

"You Can't Have My Pennies"

Not everyone maintained loyalty, and for those too young or too new to have established deep ties, MAQ was not the only masjid in town. In 2014, I went with my family to eat at a popular food market in South Central. As I walked up to a vendor to order a cupcake for my daughter, I heard, "Hey, Pam! As-salaam alaikum." I turned around to find Sister Aliyah, a younger sister whom I hadn't seen at MAQ in a while but with whom I used to chat about university life. She was a master's student at USC, working on a degree in film studies. Aliyah tended to dress more conservatively than other sisters at MAQ, and today was no different. She wore a long black tunic over black pants and a heavy black cloth head scarf that covered her hair, ears, and neck. I reintroduced Aliyah to my then three-year-old daughter. She told my daughter that she remembered her as a little baby and before that when she was in her mommy's tummy. My daughter said hi and then gleefully ran back to our table to eat her treat, leaving me alone with Aliyah.

We chatted for a while about school and work, our conversation eventually turning to the Muslim community. Aliyah said she was now going to Masjid al-Islam, an African American–led masjid in South Central with younger leadership. As we continued to talk, she confessed that she hadn't been there in a few months either.

"Why?" I asked.

"Same old politics." Then, smiling, she added, "Gotta go in, get my God, and go." I asked if she would visit MAQ during Ramadan, but she didn't plan to. She said the last time she attended, leaders had a canister out, raising money for "some construction fund." I'd seen the five-gallon plastic water jug she was referring to on a past visit. Aliyah chuckled, "You can't fool me again. . . . You can't have my pennies. I need my pennies."

Whether or not leaders actually skimmed from masjid coffers or used members' pennies for their own interests is less important on a sociological level than members' perceptions of corruption that pervaded their dealings with leaders and the consequences of these perceptions on community life, including how distrust pushed believers like Aliyah and Asaad to leave. Nor is it as important as the fact that the community as a whole preferred to keep its imam and masjid administration the same despite its suspicions. Importantly, Aliyah was younger than most MAQ members and, though born Muslim, an outsider to both Los Angeles and South Central. She was less integrated into the networks of exchange and cooperation that defined social relations at MAQ. Neither did she need these networks to the same degree. As an elite-educated woman with no children to support, Aliyah had less incentive to deepen her ties, because she saw a future with greater job opportunities. By contrast, Asaad could not escape MAQ entirely despite his frustrations and embarrassments. His family was too tied to the organization and its networks of support for him to avoid interacting with Khalid or other foes in the community.

In her classic ethnography of a low-income community in the Midwest, anthropologist Carol Stack showed that exchanges among family and friends in "the Flats" were characterized by both trust *and* distrust. The deeper the degree of entanglement, the more obligatory the ties and the greater the risk involved.[24] But, as Stack argued, the intensity of exchange would not continue "if distrust predominated over all other attitudes toward personal relations."[25] A similar pattern characterized ties at MAQ, with believers willing to risk trusting one another because they hoped to change their lives for the better. Entrepreneurialism, fed through the narrative of "do for self," made competition an expected part of religious community life. Through exchanges, believers worked out who could be relied on (or not) and who was a *good* Muslim. In this way, halal exchanges worked to "define the web of social relationships" at MAQ, operating by a logic that prioritized loyalty and shared history.[26] Without the struggles members had endured, which glued them together, the MAQ community likely would not have been able to survive the money scandals of 2012 and 2013.

∗ ∗ ∗

The narrative of "do for self" is a hopeful one, giving members a sense of greater control over their financial struggles. It fits into a longer American myth that the way out of poverty is through hard work and pulling oneself up by the bootstraps.[27] It's precisely because of this myth that "do for self" is attractive. The majority of Americans, regardless of race, are "strongly disposed to the idea that individuals are largely responsible for their own economic situations."[28] This helps explain why believers who were never in the Nation of Islam, like Sister Ava, also internalized a narrative of individual action as the means to overcome hardship. When they experienced moderate amounts of success, believers wanted to see their accomplishments as the result of hard work. And in the many more moments when they found themselves unable to earn enough, they needed to believe a brighter future was around the corner with just a little more work. This is what sociologist Arlie Hochschild calls the "deep story"—the story that removes fact and judgment to tap into how things feel.[29] It *feels* better to most Americans to believe we have the power to achieve our dreams, but it obscures forces outside our control that limit our capacities for action.

For his part, Fareed thought members were holding back, telling me, "People who come here got money. They got money. But they hearts ain't in the right place." It was a declaration about the misplaced intentions of believers unwilling to put care for the community over care of self. Fareed expressed to me his frustration with the masjid's inabilities to pay its bills, often doing so when we were hanging out together in the office. He had a hard shell, but from our private conversations I knew that he cared deeply for the community and its fragile future. This care motivated his sometimes harsh management style, like the brisk way he called out "Shut the door!" to prevent heat from escaping the building during winter or cool air during summer. He was afraid of even small amounts of waste. Running a masjid with too few resources to meet community needs and demands requires persistence—or *tinkering*, as a prominent anthropologist of care has argued.[30] That's why even if believers can't eliminate the pain of inequality, a good Muslim in this setting keeps trying, keeps tinkering.

CHAPTER FOUR

"Why Not Just Use a Cucumber!"

"I need a shirt that says on the front, I Am Not Here to Look for a Man." Sisters Roxanne and Aisha were sitting together on the floor inside the masjid. When I joined the women with my plate, Roxanne was telling Aisha that the brothers' mouths started watering when they saw her get out of the car with her catering pans.

"Hey, you never know," I teased. "Nailah also said there wasn't a man down here for her, and look now."

Almost in unison the sisters replied, "But he's not from here!"

"No, but she *met* him here." I was referring to Aisha's daughter, Sister Nailah, who met a man at Masjid al-Quran whom she would later date and marry. The man lived in New York and had been visiting as part of an event.

Sitting up straighter, Roxanne said, "Okay, I concede your point." Almost immediately, though, she relaxed back into a more casual way of talking, saying how the "men down here" were "no good." She added, "Brothers down here say, 'Get on welfare, sister, stay at home, sister.'" Roxanne's comment referred to the idea that men and women could have an Islamic marriage that was religiously binding but not legal by US laws—and therefore not a marriage that would nullify government benefits to single mothers.

Men at MAQ portrayed themselves as protectors and providers, and they tended to proclaim that women are the keepers of the home. As one of the imams instructed in his khutbah, "Be kind to womenfolk. It's their duty to be chaste and good, and ours to be good to them." This kind of essentializing gender discourse, combined with institutionalized gender segregation and the exclusion of women from religious leadership in most mosques around the world, contributes to public perceptions of Islam as an innately patriarchal religion that suppresses women's interests.[1] As anthropologist Saba Mahmood so eloquently explained, any study of Muslim women must at some point engage with "all the assumptions this dubious signifier triggers in the Western imagination concerning Islam's patriarchal and misogynist qualities."[2]

To a certain extent, women at MAQ accepted and even promoted traditional gender roles, but idealized notions of men as providers clashed with the lived reality that many of these women experienced. More often, the sisters worked and supported their families, while brothers struggled to find and keep employment. Many men suffered the stigma and material mark of a criminal record, or they lacked the education and experience to compete for well-paying jobs.[3] I knew only a handful who worked in the kind of job that could support a family in an expensive city like Los Angeles. Men's failure to provide for their wives and the tensions this produced were both a recurrent source of marital tension and legitimate grounds for divorce in women's eyes.

This chapter examines how the MAQ community tried to valorize traditional gender roles in order to strengthen African American Muslim families. It also examines how the women, in response to perceptions that brothers failed to live up to their ideal roles within Islam, came together to create stronger gendered social support networks. The result was women in the community being able to go beyond relying on one another for material survival to become their own agent of protection and security.[4] The urban-racial structure of everyday life in South Central is such that women at MAQ become compelled to frame Islam as a source of relief from having to do it all as Black women. It's a relief they don't always find; but their disappointment, in turn, has pushed them to create sisterhood networks that give a deeper sense of religious community and gendered racial strength. And while the men continue to dominate religious authority inside the mosque, the women clearly see themselves as better off than men.

"None Stood as Tall as Clara Muhammad"

Like any religious organization, the masjid existed chiefly as a place of worship, and in this capacity men dominated at MAQ.[5] Only men served as imams, giving khutbahs and leading congregational prayer. Only men performed the *adhan* (call to prayer), a sacred duty of additional symbolic importance in this setting, because the first muezzin in Islamic history was a former African slave. Men also taught all official religious classes and controlled access to masjid finances.[6] The latter was no small source of power given the community's shared material needs. Male leaders could determine how the community spent its limited money, including which events would be catered, while women generally had to raise funds for their own events. For brothers-only conferences and meetings, women served lunch and organized administrative tasks for brothers. For sisters-only events, brothers sometimes provided security. Most times, though, only sisters organized for and served other women. Within this patriarchal structure, women's work tended to be domestic (e.g., cooking, cleaning, decorating), and the few sisters with official office roles handled mostly secretarial tasks. The work performed by women also received less formal recognition than that of brothers. Moreover, men outnumbered women at nearly every religious service, be it jumah, iftar, or Taraweeh.

The organization of the masjid reflected a traditional gender ideology reinforced in religious teachings. In their khutbahs and lectures, men stressed that women are to be validated for their care work of family. This is captured best in how imams at MAQ spoke about the legend of Sister Clara Muhammad, wife of Nation of Islam founder Elijah Muhammad and mother of W. D. Mohammed. In one lecture, Imam Khalid told his community, "Dear Believers, we can't overlook the role of African American women." He named Sojourner Truth and Harriet Tubman as exemplars of women who had advanced the interests of Black communities, also recognizing "European-American women who helped," such as Eleanor Roosevelt. And among these great women, Imam Khalid declared that "none stood as tall as Clara Muhammad." Clara was the reason her family entered Islam. She persuaded her husband to hear Wallace Fard, the peddler turned prophet who would later allow him to assume Nation leadership. She also supported her husband during his entanglements with the law, even befriending a prison guard so that Muhammad could secure a blackboard for educating inmates and bring them into the faith. It was the beginning of the Nation's famous prison ministry, Iman Khalid explained, and a practice of *dawah* (outreach) that continues at MAQ and in many other African American Muslim communities. Given the number of men at MAQ who had criminal records, Khalid's decision to highlight this aspect of Clara's story was a reminder to the sisters that their role to support men does not stop in times of forced separation.

* * *

Sister Clara Muhammad's dedication to her family and faith mirrors a common narrative of struggle among pious Black women—hope for a better future while working to make do in the present. When Clara met Fard in the 1930s, she was, in the words of Muslim feminist historian Debra Majeed, "searching for a tangible anchor in an environment where many disillusioned Blacks hunger[ed] for a religion that spoke to their 'material reality.'"[7] The family had moved to Detroit from their native Georgia in 1923 and, like many migrants from the South, found the North to be an unwelcoming place. Employers openly discriminated against Black workers, and the threat of violence from race riots provoked families' sense of unease. On top of these troubles were the struggles to make do amid difficult living conditions. In "An Invitation to 22 Million Black Americans" published in 1967 in the NOI's newspaper *Muhammad Speaks*, Clara described the family's "lowest ebb," writing, "With five children, there were times we didn't have a piece of bread in the house, nor heat, water or even sufficient wearing apparel. My husband would walk the streets looking for a job daily, but would come home with no job."[8] She started working as a domestic servant to support her family, but her husband disliked seeing his wife go to work in an industry where Black women suffered regular sexual and physical violence.[9] So when the family entered the Nation and Elijah Muhammad later took over the movement, Clara welcomed its ideals of patriarchy and respectability, because her husband's new role "liberated" her from having to "rescue" him.[10] It is this liberation that helps attract African American women to Islam to this day.[11]

As a leader, Muhammad espoused both conservative and contradictory positions on the roles that women should occupy. According to experts on women in the Nation, his gender ideology was "influenced by and symptomatic of a postwar mass culture that tied women to the domestic sphere."[12] On the other hand, as with most of Muhammad's teachings, these views exhibited an intersectional awareness that recognized the particularities of being a Muslim woman who is Black. For Muhammad, race provided the primary lens for making sense of social life. He stressed that Black women should be protected from "the devil white race" that has sexualized and assaulted them since slavery. Through his writings and the Muslim Girl Training classes required of sisters in the Nation, women were instructed to dress modestly, cook clean foods, avoid sex outside marriage, and submit to their husbands. Given Muhammad's strong displeasure with white society, it's ironic that "the NOI adhered to Victorian ideals of respectability and chastity."[13]

"Paradise Lies at the Feet of the Mother"

Respectability and chastity remained central to the qualities of the ideal African American Muslim woman after the thousands of NOI members transitioned to Sunni Islam, but with a far less misogynistic bent. When Imam Mohammed took over for his father, the new leader turned to both the Qur'an and his mother's legacy to develop a revised gender ideology.[14]

Mohammed said his mother's upbringing in the church was instrumental in showing him how a Black woman could live a pious life, distinguishing herself from less respectable women. In "Researching Our Faith for the Business Life in Our Neighborhoods," a public lecture given to his followers in 2006 in Homewood, Illinois, Imam Mohammed said, "My mother . . . didn't use drugs, she didn't smoke, she didn't drink liquors, and she wore long dresses . . . she didn't make any vulgar or indecent display of her-self—*before* she became a follower of the Honorable Elijah Muhammad. She was a decent church woman."[15] With his words, Mohammed reinforced a dominant discourse that the Black urban community is divided between "decent" and "street" behaviors.[16]

Given the obvious adoration Mohammed had for his mother, it's not surprising that his teachings concerning gender focused on women's roles as mothers. In his 1976 publication *The Man and the WoMan in Islam*, Mohammed wrote, "Society begins growing in the womb of the mother. . . . In one of his sayings, [the] Prophet Muhammad tells us in plain words that the future of heaven of the society depends upon how the mother raises the little children that are at her feet."[17] Here Mohammed referenced a popu-lar hadith: *Paradise lies at the feet of the mother*. According to Dawn-Marie Gibson and Jamillah Karim, Mohammed viewed women as spiritually and intellectually equal to men but "as having distinct, though equally regarded, natures," and he directly criticized (white) feminism as undermining the natural abilities of women to excel as caregivers.[18] "Women's lib' is not an accident," Imam Mohammed stated in a 1977 lecture.[19] "It is a divine thing but women have to rise above the 'lib' to understand that we want more than just lip. We want mothers who have mothers' hearts."[20] He argued that a pro-women stance should also be pro-men in order to be Islamic, describing the roles of both in essentialized terms: "Some things a man can do and it's his natural role to do those things. If you (women) will admit the truth you know that it's not in you to jump up and go out and fight a physical enemy. It's not your nature. God didn't put that in your nature. Your nature is love. You want to protect your home life."[21]

Mohammed also said that by protecting the home, women would be protecting the best of what humanity has developed. He continued, "I'm trying to promote women's lib and at the same time *save society*."[22] Moham-med taught that women should contribute to society at large through their care work as wives and mothers, reinforcing the idea that sisters are freer when they can devote themselves to their families without being beholden to the demands of financially supporting them. In this way, he addressed the multiple ways in which Black women have been held back from their "natural" roles, combining gender essentialism with elements of intersec-tional feminism.

Imam Mohammed's interpretations of the Qur'an and his teachings often took on "a womanist quality."[23] Womanist theology accounts for the interlocking systems of race, class, and gender oppression that shape Black women's lives, and it posits that theology speaks best to them when it accounts for experiences with racism and sexism. In addition, it provides a way of addressing suffering through scripture.[24] The "collective religious ethos" that womanist theology promotes appealed especially to African American Muslim women, because it offered a way of thinking about women and men's *shared* survival. According to critical race scholar Sylvia Chan-Malik, feminism asserts equality between the sexes, whereas African American Islam promotes *complementarity*.[25] For many Muslim women "feminism demeans women's esteemed roles as wives and mothers in Islam."[26] They point out that Islam already grants women explicit rights to own property, work outside the home, and manage their own finances.[27] In this view, "men and women are equal before God yet should not strive to perform the same tasks or occupy the same roles in society."[28]

✳   ✳   ✳

Religious leaders at MAQ promoted a gender ideology similar to that of Imam Mohammed. An MAQ-produced brochure about Islam that I picked up in 2017 stated, "Muslims do not believe women are morally, spiritually, or intellectually inferior to men. Both of them have *unique and equitable roles* in Muslim community life and society."[29] Here the masjid advanced a "separate but equal" approach to gender within Islam, enforcing the idea that a healthy religious community is one in which women and men occupy *separate spheres*, with men as economic providers and women as homemakers and caregivers who adhere to a *cult of domesticity*.[30] Dawn Marie Dow explains, "The cult of domesticity emphasizes that women should exemplify four key virtues: piety, purity, submissiveness, and domesticity."[31] For some Black women, especially those in lower economic strata who had been working outside the home their entire lives, hearing a religious leader explicitly link piety to separate spheres and a cult of domesticity appealed as a new kind of twenty-first-century liberation — one that extends beyond the self. The goal of a stable family at MAQ was thus to create a more stable community.[32]

This explains why motherhood constituted one of the most important ways in which women were seen as contributing to the community. Children were considered blessings from Allah, and throughout their history in the Nation and Sunni Islam, women at MAQ put significant value in bearing children. It was not unusual for me to meet a woman with seven or more children, well above the national average of 1.8 births per woman.

Women also commonly helped raise or care for grandchildren and step-children, further expanding their kin networks. Sister Ava bragged that she raised not just her seven biological children but the niece of an ex-partner, an ex-girlfriend of one of her sons, and a grandchild (who was a high school student and living in Ava's house when I started fieldwork). A Black woman in South Central boasting that she raised ten children and framing this as a measure of her moral worth was no diminutive act. It constituted a politically charged assault on dominant discourses about Black motherhood.

Most members of the MAQ community were old enough to have lived through the controversial Moynihan Report and to have experienced its impacts on social policy in low-income communities. The 1965 report presented the behaviors of African American men and women as a set of "ghetto pathologies" that had contributed to the disproportionate number of social, economic, and political problems found in low-income Black communities in the United States.[33] The report "marshalled social psychological stereotypes of Black men as fallen, emasculated men, motivated almost completely by masculine strivings."[34] And rather than situate women's actions to support their families in a context of economic struggles, Black women became framed as a central part of the problem by emasculating Black men.[35] The so-called breakdown of the Black family then became a guiding force in social policy and research.

Subsequent social science research has tended to reinforce controlling images of Black women as matriarchs who fail to conform to appropriate gender behavior.[36] According to Patricia Hill Collins, "Much social science research implicitly uses gender relations in African-American communities as one seeming measure of Black cultural disadvantage."[37] Within this research, "black family structures are seen as being deviant because they challenge the patriarchal assumptions underpinning the traditional family ideal. Moreover, the absence of Black patriarchy is used as evidence for Black cultural inferiority."[38] The MAQ community's efforts to valorize traditional gender roles must be understood within this context of controlling images. Such images work to make racism and sexism appear "natural, normal, and inevitable parts of everyday life."[39] By turning motherhood from a cause of inequality into a prized role that deepens individual worth and lifts up the community, believers find a way to "flip the script" on negative stereotypes of urban-dwelling Black families.

At the same time, believers' efforts to promote traditional gender norms puts sisters in conversation with another set of controlling images, those of Muslim women as oppressed and in need of saving.[40] Chan-Malik explains, "The Poor Muslim Woman is a static and essentialized trope that is deployed to justify U.S. military attacks and military occupation in the Middle

East, the profiling and surveillance of Muslim communities in the United States, even the notion of 'banning' Muslims altogether from the country."[41] In the context of African American Islam and historical discourses about the Nation of Islam, Chan-Malik has shown that underneath the trope of the Poor Muslim Woman is an idea that her "submission" may be interpreted as a result of the "brutal power of the Muslim men who controlled her."[42]

Most believers at MAQ have non-Muslim family they spend time with or even live alongside. These relatives may push back against the idea that women's work is chiefly in the care of the home. One of Ava's blood sisters scoffed at any woman who would choose "His-lam," and plenty more family members expressed similarly disparaging comments about the religion. One rather vocal niece blamed Islam for changing the fun, free-spirited Avaline into the pious, boring Sister Ava. Ava thought her family misunderstood the religion and, for the most part, ignored their complaints.

The sisters at MAQ exist somewhere in the middle of all these competing images, navigating a murky gender terrain. They must contend with stereotypes not only of Black women as *too strong* but also of Muslim women as *too weak*. From their lived experiences, they know they can handle struggle, but they don't use an explicitly feminist frame to understand their actions. They stay focused on the pragmatics of fulfilling their material, emotional, and sexual needs.

In light of the multiple constraints women at MAQ have faced over the community's long history, it seems likely that its leaders have been romanticizing gender roles of past decades. Indeed, Dawn-Marie Gibson and Jamillah Karim show in their historical analysis of narratives of former and current Nation of Islam members that sisters have always resisted leaders' attempts to restrict women to the home.[43] In the same way, sisters at MAQ wanted to be honored for their roles as wives and mothers but not limited to them. Many dreamed aloud of plans to establish businesses or pursue formal degrees. Sister Dina, wife of the head imam, worked long hours as a school administrator with dreams of opening her own charter school. She wasn't content to live off her husband's income—indeed it's possible he didn't earn enough to pay their rent or car notes (with no formal accounting records, we can't know).

Still, I think it's fair to say that many more women envied Sister Aisha's status as a full-time mother than that of women who worked outside the home. Sisters admired Aisha's large family, stable living conditions, and fashionable style. She maintained this revered status among sisters even after her husband moved out of state and she stayed in LA alone to care for their family, in part because he continued to provide financial support. Anthropologist Carolyn Rouse, who spent years studying the lives of African American Muslim women in Los Angeles, describes African American Muslim women as tired of having to "do it all." "They want relief from having to bring in an income and manage all domestic affairs. Many women would like men to have a comparable desire for family stability, and if performing gender is the method to achieve that goal, so be it."[44]

In other words, the question is not why women at MAQ support a gender ideology that portrays marriage as freedom. Rather, it's *why not* support a gender ideology that promotes a path to fewer financial burdens, especially when the weight of the world falls on your shoulders? The "freedom" to stay at home has never been available to Black women in the United States except for an elite few.[45] At the same time, African American Muslim women approach gender roles in Islam with a heavy dose of pragmatism.[46] So a traditional division of rights and responsibilities makes sense if it strengthens the family, but if men fail to uphold their end of the bargain, an African American Muslim woman accepts divorce as a reasonable consequence.

"I Divorce You, I Divorce You, I Divorce You"

For all their jokes that they wouldn't marry a brother from Masjid al-Quran, sisters did sometimes get married to men they met there. Sister Amina was one of them. She met a brother early into Ramadan one year and started talking with him. A few days later, I heard they got married.

As the weeks of Ramadan wore on, the man became a bit of a joke among the sisters. He was a large man but too soft-spoken to be deemed strong. Sisters rolled their eyes at him, which he took calmly. Amina, by contrast, had a voice that betrayed her slim form. You may not have heard what her husband said, but you heard Amina loud and clear. Unsurprisingly to her friends, the couple started having marital troubles fairly soon into their union. They asked Imam Khalid to counsel them, which he did one evening that same Ramadan inside the masjid. Everyone sitting outside that evening could hear Amina screaming. A sister who needed Amina to take her home to the halfway house she had been paroled to and where she had a strict curfew of 11:00 p.m. stood nervously, glancing at the time on her phone. She was too afraid of Amina's anger to interrupt. It was 10:40, and Sister Ava said she'd had enough. She went and banged on the door, saw Imam Khalid "beggin'" her "with his eyes" for help, and marched inside. "Amina, that girl needs you to take her home. *Now.*" Amina stormed out of the masjid and drove off in such a fury, everyone stopped to watch her compact car kicking up gravel. "What's wrong with her?" someone in the crowd asked.

As a group of sisters dissected the incident the next night, Sister Natalie commented, "I don't know if it was a real marriage or one of those 'I marry you' three times."

"I marry you, I marry you, I marry you," Aisha chimed in. The women were referring to a disputed practice of instant and often temporary marriage, sometimes called pleasure marriages or Nikah mut'ah in Islamic studies. These unions are extrajudicial, meaning they occur outside state legal systems, and they take place largely to maintain sexual propriety.

Natalie said she was disappointed with these "young sisters" who "think with their butts, not their heads." Well into her eighties, Natalie thought everyone under the age of sixty was young. She commented aloud that she didn't understand why Amina married the guy.

"Because she needed to get some," Ava stated matter-of-factly.

Natalie jumped on that. "Why not just use a cucumber!" We all turned to Natalie, her usually no-nonsense scowl giving way to the beginnings of a cheeky smile. Sister Ava and I had tears in our eyes when we finally stopped laughing.

*   *   *

Six days after their well-publicized counseling session, I was standing next to Amina in the iftar line when her husband came up and asked if he could have a word. She told him "Not now," but he kept pushing. Through gritted teeth, Amina repeated, "Not now."

He wouldn't go away and instead asked, "Why is it every time I look up, you talkin' to him?"

"No, you didn't." Now Amina was really pissed. "Are you kidding me? Get away." He walked off, and she ate at the sisters' table without him, continuing a trend I had observed since their wedding.

When dinner was over but Taraweeh prayers had not yet started, Amina marched over to her car and pulled something small out of it. Then she came back and tugged on Aisha's shoulder and touched Fareed's arm. She asked whether they could "come in the house" with her. The three of them hadn't even reached the office steps when Amina stopped. A small crowd had formed and in the darkness I couldn't see exactly what was happening, but not thirty seconds later Aisha started walking back. She announced that Amina had gotten divorced.

"What do you mean?" I asked.

"Amina told him, 'I divorce you, I divorce you, I divorce you.'" Aisha imitated pushing something into the guy's chest and then quickly walking away. The sisters standing with us surmised that Amina probably gave the man some money to leave her alone. With that, her marriage was over.

The declaration "I divorce you" three times is Amina's enactment of a highly controversial practice called triple *talaq*, or instant divorce. It typically refers to a husband's ability to end a marriage simply by repudiating it.[47] News reports tell of wives receiving a triple talaq without warning, including one case in which an Indian woman said her husband, a school principal, divorced her over WhatsApp.[48] In a triple talaq, a wife is stripped of her marital status without her consent, often causing her shame and hardship.[49] Divorce can limit or erase a man's financial obligations, undermining a woman's economic well-being. Critics argue that triple talaq is more a patriarchal holdover from pre-Islamic times than anything validated by Islamic exegesis, but in several countries the extrajudicial practice continues with implicit, if not explicit, legal protection in Islamic courts. Many Muslim clerics in India, for example, say the practice of instant divorce is morally reprehensible, but they are unwilling to invalidate a triple talaq.[50] Muslim feminists and women legal scholars have called for governments to abolish triple talaq in the interest of promoting women's rights in Islamic societies.[51]

Yet here it was a woman enacting a triple talaq. Amina thus appropriated a patriarchal practice to suit *her* sexual and religious interests. She was instrumental throughout the processes of entering and leaving the marriage. Plus she wasn't afraid for her marital struggles or divorce to become public, casting aside the idea that she should feel shame. I do not wish to imply that a triple talaq divorce was common in the community—at least not one declared so openly. However, the agentic force with which Amina enacted her wishes—both the desire to fulfill a religious intention and the businesslike style of resolving a problem that emerged in the enactment of that intention—exemplifies how women approached gender roles in Islam. The calm reaction of observing sisters also underscores women's religious pragmatism: they weren't surprised Amina would marry in seeming haste, but neither did they get worked up when she divorced. They assumed Amina had given some sort of monetary settlement, indicating they saw her as the breadwinner and holding a power that the man did not have.

My ability to speak about Amina's reasons for marrying this specific man is limited. She was difficult to get along with and I kept my distance. Natalie, who relied on Amina for rides, described her fellow Muslima this way: "She's a good person, but she's mean." Still, from the interactions I had with Amina and those I observed, I think it's fair to say she took Islam seriously—*very* seriously. She wasn't afraid to approach an imam when she disagreed with his teaching, and she complained loudly when she saw something happening at MAQ that she deemed un-Islamic. So it wasn't surprising that she wanted to get married or that she was willing to do it with such zeal—even if only to protect her chastity. Nor did it surprise anyone when she applied the same zeal to getting out of marriage.

*   *   *

Amina's breakup was exceptionally dramatic, but even she tried to make her marriage work by seeking Imam Khalid's counsel. The strong pressure to be married came not only from others in the community but also from within. Sister Verna joined the Nation of Islam in 1993 and later transitioned to Sunni Islam at another African American–led masjid. She started coming to MAQ because of her husband. They had been married eight years when I met her. "Phew, it has not been easy!" she told me during that first conversation. If not for her *din* (faith), she said she wouldn't be married. If you're going to marry, Verna explained, it was best to marry someone "you have more in common than different." She used education as an example from her own marriage as a difference that caused conflict. "I hear from him all the time, 'Oh, you're educated.'" She said she told him it doesn't matter if you have an education, because what's more important is being able to self-educate. Verna encouraged her husband to learn how to take charge of his contractor business. But he didn't. She told me of coming home from her job as a nurse and finding him with his feet up, watching TV. Frustrations continued for several years, until the death of her father left her with properties to manage and a greater sense of freedom. After that, Verna split from her husband and stopped attending MAQ.

Sisters go into marriage with high hopes, but the political economy in South Central is such that brothers in the community often cannot live up to the qualities of the ideal Muslim husband. For some men, it becomes impossible to hide their financial struggles. Two brothers lived on the masjid grounds full-time, one with a room inside the office cottage and the other with official permission to park his RV on the lot. I observed other brothers living at MAQ off and on, including one young man who lived inside the prayer hall for approximately six months. Sisters, on the other hand, did not have official permission to live or sleep at the masjid, resulting in a less equitable distribution of this specific social service the mosque provided its struggling community.[52] Of course, with men's domestication of the masjid comes the public revelation of their private struggle to provide for themselves. And if they can't earn enough for housing, it's not a far leap for sisters to assume that these brothers can't provide for a wife. That was why Sister Roxanne described the men down at MAQ as "no good" even as she remained committed to attending an African American–led masjid in a low-income urban community.

"If You Can't Say Anything Nice about Anybody, Come Sit by Me"

Sisters recognized the limited job opportunities faced by men in South Central. In some ways, they were more forgiving of the men's economic failings than brothers were of one another. But neither were sisters willing to sacrifice their ideal Muslim husband for the marriage pool that lay directly in front of them. Their response, like that of generations of women in low-income communities, was to turn to one another to create gendered support networks.[53] These networks allowed them to better meet their material needs and fulfill their roles as caregivers when financial assistance from a partner was not available. For example, Sister Haleema owned a large home a few miles west of MAQ. She loaned out extra bedrooms to sisters without a place to stay, including those who had left their husband or lost their job. She also helped brothers in need of housing, but men had to pay to rent one of her other properties. It would have been inappropriate for the unmarried Haleema to let a brother stay in her home. Likewise, brothers without a place to stay did not crash with married couples. But when a sister with serious mental health problems became homeless, a couple let her live in their one-bedroom apartment for several months.[54] In other words, sisters didn't need to live at MAQ, because they had other places they could go when down on their luck.

Sisters also helped one another with child care, serving as caregivers in the masjid and as babysitters when needed. On Fridays and at special events, it was difficult to identify which child belonged to whom: the masjid grounds became a makeshift playground patrolled by brothers but supervised by sisters. When a sleeping baby woke up and started crying, it wasn't unusual for a nearby sister to pick up the child and rock it back to sleep. The trust that sisters cultivated with one another may not have extended to business dealings, as I explored in chapter 3, but when it came to matters involving children, they could generally count on one another for support.

The Muslima network that sisters have cultivated enabled them to survive without relying on men, but the network went further, because the sisters wanted more needs met than material ones. They wanted love, friendship, comradery, security, a sense of belonging—and many more rewards of a rich social life. They committed to make this happen with or without men but, importantly, not without Islam. They turned to one another to form meaningful sisterhood networks and in so doing deepened their din. It was often the women who had the worst experiences with marriage who were most committed to making the masjid a safe space of sisterhood.

*   *   *

Sister Ava's phone lit up with a new message. Her sons were texting "Happy Father's Day" wishes. She said she'd been both their mother and their father as they were growing up—a realization she'd had while still young. She had her first child at the age of sixteen and dropped out of high school soon afterward. Though she and the father later married and had more children together, he was an alcoholic and the marriage didn't last. She had another serious relationship that was fun but volatile. Ava referred to this ex-partner as her "sperm donor," because he never paid child support. To make ends meet, she worked multiple jobs at one time, often off the books, so she could continue to receive food stamps, Medicaid, and other government benefits. She taught herself how to turn fifty dollars' worth of food stamps into cake she'd bake, slice, and sell for twice that amount. Yet every time Ava mastered one hardship, another surfaced. The sperm donor once turned her in to authorities for working while receiving welfare, and Ava had to educate herself on the system in order to fight to regain her benefits.

Strive, struggle, survive, repeat. Life continued in this pattern until 1981, when Ava became a Muslim and decided to try marriage again, this time with a man from the MAQ community. She was in her early thirties, with her youngest still in training pants, and already a grandmother several times over. Two of her older sons had dropped out of school and were in "that life" (gangs and drugs), causing Ava to live in fear of the day she'd get a call that one had been shot and killed. It took tremendous energy for her to keep her daughters safe. Her informal catering and cleaning business required work at all hours, meaning she cleaned pots and baked cakes while the kids slept. In short, Ava was exhausted. Like many African American Muslim women, she was attracted to the Islamic ideal that a husband would provide and protect.[55] Her new husband worked as a sanitation engineer for the city, earning a steady paycheck and giving her access to better medical benefits.

Ava entered the marriage with high hopes and a willingness to be more submissive than she had been in previous relationships. She let her husband help steer her catering business, and together they ran a makeshift restaurant in front of their house, less than one mile from MAQ. Ava recalled Muslims coming over after jumah and sitting at the café tables on her front lawn, enjoying the LA sunshine over plates of homemade chili mac and BBQ chicken. However, as she told it, she was headstrong, and her husband suffered from past addiction demons. After relapsing, he emptied their joint bank account with the help of another brother at MAQ and spent all their savings. Then the couple split but didn't divorce so that Ava could stay on his insurance. In this way, her husband extended a lasting favor, allowing her to remain his beneficiary. When he died in 2003 shortly after his sixty-third birthday, Ava thought it was the least he could do to make her a widow. Though the union did not last, she knew she had tried to the best of her ability. In her execution of good if unfulfilled intentions, she saw herself as strengthening her commitment to Islam.

Back on her own for several years when we met in 2008 and more recently a breast cancer survivor, Ava struggled with whether to marry again. Her cooking skills made her desirable to many brothers. In the years we were close, she turned down at least two men who expressed interest in marrying her, including one brother from MAQ. She told him he was "too young" for her but in private shared that he was a recovering drug addict, and she had zero interest in going through that struggle again. The other marriage request came from an African Muslim brother who attended a nearby masjid that Ava cooked for during Ramadan. The man would have been able to provide for her—he ran a successful business—but Ava was hesitant to marry a man from Africa, fearing he would expect her to stay in the house. She was too accustomed to being able to "rip and run" on her own, and more generally she was suspicious of men who were eager to help out financially. When one of the men at MAQ offered to help her if she ever needed money, Ava thanked him but declined. She told me, "I don't want him to think I owe him." Then she explained she can get what she wants from brothers without giving *this*, pointing to her vagina. Taking five dollars from Brother Fareed in the office or accepting a tip for a catering order was OK, but accepting cash from a brother in the community with no explicit strings attached was asking for trouble.

More than relying on brothers, for help in her later years Ava turned to both her network of sisters in the Muslim community and her non-Muslim sisters. The person she relied on most was her best friend of more than thirty years, Sister Aisha. The pair were famous, known within the community to see each other nearly every day. Often the visits took place at MAQ, other times at their homes or in their travels around the neighborhood. Even after a day spent hanging out, they would call each other and talk so late into the night that Aisha regularly fell asleep with the phone to her ear. Ava could really talk. She loved to tell old stories over and over again, with Aisha patiently listening each time—even when it was the tenth, fifteenth, or twentieth time she'd heard them.

Between 2009 and 2011, Sisters Ava and Aisha generously involved me in many of their daily adventures. From my vantage point in the backseat of Ava's rusted car, I could listen and observe without intruding too much. I saw directly how the women countered their bad experiences in marriage with a strong Muslim sisterhood. Even as Ava and I grew closer and it became Aisha who was joining us rather than me tagging along, the strength of the sisters' bond shined brightly. On one memorable occasion, the three of us went to a downtown cafeteria to eat lunch with Aisha's eldest son, Asaad. We stacked our trays and retreated to a deserted section of the restaurant, where for two hours Ava and Aisha reminisced about raising children in South Central. Both remembered fondly the movie sleepovers at Ava's old house — the one she lost because of her ex-husband. The children set up a fort in the living room and everyone camped out, watching movies through the night. Asaad joked that he watched *Willow* way too many times, because Ava loved the fantasy film about a magical land. Ava liked to say she was the Huckleberry Finn of South Central, and even in her sixties boasted that she had the heart of a child. She brought a much-needed dose of fun and laughter to Aisha's stern household, and she earned an invitation to most of Aisha's family functions — a rare privilege given the family's tight-knit nature.

Movie nights continued after the children left home, but now the women were setting up in the masjid. Ava carried a portable TV with built-in DVD player, hooking it up via an extension cord she kept in her trunk. That way, she could put the TV in the right spot in the prayer hall and the sisters could lean against a wall to watch, tucking themselves under thick blankets. I knew I was officially part of the crew when Ava bought a blanket for me from a vendor she knew in downtown LA. She told me to keep it in my trunk so I'd always be prepared whenever we'd need a movie night. Some weeks, we went down to the masjid three or four nights in a row.

We watched all kinds of movies, but romantic comedies were a favorite. One night, Ava brought a scratchy DVD of *Steel Magnolias*, the 1989 classic "chick flick" about a group of Southern women who gather in a beauty shop in preparation for a wedding. The film featured an all-star, all-white cast: Julia Roberts, Shirley MacLaine, Olympia Dukakis, Dolly Parton, Sally Field. At first glance, there wasn't much about its setting or plot that should have appealed to a Black woman living in South Central LA, but the sense of sisterhood it glamorized and the way that women formed the core of their tight-knit Southern community were irresistible to Ava. She loved the film and watched it several times. Shirley MacLaine's character, Ouiser, says in the movie: "A dirty mind is a terrible thing to waste." It reminded me of Ava's saucy mouth, and the classy, delightfully sarcastic character Clairee reminded me of Aisha. "If you can't say anything nice about anybody, come sit by me," Clairee tells Truvy, the beauty shop operator. Like this character, Aisha kept her cards close to her chest, so you wouldn't know she had a biting sense of humor unless she allowed you to get close to her. For a while, I even used the names of the two characters as pseudonyms for Ava and Aisha in my field notes to remember the fun we had that night and how the characters captured unique elements about each woman.

Before the movies began, we usually grabbed something to eat from a nearby fast-food restaurant or grocery store, unwrapping our burritos or dipping our chips on plates we'd spread out on the prayer hall rug. Our conversations during dinner touched on a range of subjects: gossip about the MAQ community, developments in the sisters' non-Muslim families, cooking, politics, celebrities. Rarely did we discuss religion per se, but I learned a great deal about how the sisters understood Islam through these conversations. Talking about your religious community is part of how you make sense of what religion is and your role as a woman in it. I came to regard these movie nights as a form of informal religious education because of the conversations they generated about faith and community. The masjid administration didn't like our activities, commenting to Ava that some people thought it haram to eat and watch movies in the prayer hall, but none of the leaders tried too hard to stop us (and if they had, Ava and Aisha would have ignored them).

Through the women's decades of raising children together in the community, Ava brought out a playful side of Aisha hidden to most other people, and Aisha provided Ava a willing ear to talk through struggles. Within this safe space inside the masjid, where the women could tease, criticize, and laugh about the people and things happening in their lives, they developed trust and complementary styles of humor. Their movie nights constitute a form of Black placemaking that sustains, affirms, and brings pleasure to the women.[56] As Marcus Hunter and colleagues recently pointed out, "Black placemaking refers to the ways that urban Black Americans create sites of endurance, belonging, and resistance."[57] This practice has sustained the women through the stresses of everyday life; and with the expectation that they could rely on each other for comfort and companionship, they felt safer in the neighborhood and more connected to their Muslim community.

Ava's refusal to remarry, Aisha's preference to remain in LA when her husband moved, and the bond these women created that was stronger than marriage bring me to a larger point about the pragmatic gender ideology of the sisters at MAQ. Women there are accustomed to doing things on their own—so much so that even when men can provide for them, sisters are sometimes hesitant or flat out resistant. After a while, they find themselves wanting to be free of having to deal with men as partners, finding it more rewarding to rely on one another and their wider sisterhood networks. Sister Natalie's joke that a woman could get what she needed with a cucumber instead of a man captures precisely how women approached gender roles at MAQ: recognize your needs and be prepared to handle them on your own. And you better do it with humor. This latter point is key to understanding the lives of the women at MAQ and a central part of the community's overall ethos toward living and worshipping in South Central. Life was hard—to the extent that food and housing weren't guaranteed—but laughter proved to be a productive strategy for dealing with many of the maddening aspects of life in South Central. As deep and dark as things may have seemed in tense moments, there were more tears from laughter than sadness, at least when the sisters got together. This is the beauty of a safe space and why the mosque was a place of relief for them.

"Get Up There and Tell Him You Want It!"

At Masjid al-Quran, women are idealists about Islam and pragmatists about gender. We see this clearly in their decision-making around marriage, which they interpret as required in Islam but frame as required only when a man lives up to his obligations. When a husband lets his wife down, it's perfectly reasonable for her to move to protect her moral and material interests. In other words, the women ensure that their understandings of Islam account for the lived reality of being Black women living in an urban environment where men can't always provide. They infuse a certain urban-racial pragmatism into their piety. No one gets what they say they want, but both women and men get to continue to create an Islam that offers hope for future change. It is a form of dynamic agency, one that starts on a certain path with a set of intentions and must change in response to larger structures of race, class, and gender. It should not be reduced to "adaptation," as the literature on urban poverty tends to do, nor is faith engaged here as a mere "coping mechanism."[58]

The ways that women in the MAQ community have carved out a safe space to accommodate their needs and desires allow them to separate themselves, physically and symbolically, from the many unsafe social spaces to which Black women have been subjugated throughout US history.[59] So even if the organization of the mosque is "far from ideal," it remains a spiritual structure that supports, nurtures, and validates them.[60] Consistent with other conservative religious women, sisters at MAQ do not reject ideas that promote women's interests, although "their solutions, agendas, movements, and motivations may not align with standard definitions of feminism."[61] Instead, they posit a traditional interpretation of gender roles within Islam as the best framework for finding solutions to the problems Black communities face, sometimes with consequences of being perceived as oppressed.

If Ava's family thought Muslim women were too meek, they clearly had never talked with Sisters Natalie or Amina. In fact, most of the women I met at MAQ were anything but meek, and they worked conceptions of strength into their roles as Muslim women. This became clearer to me as my years in the community ticked on and sisters took me under their wing. They taught that I would need to stand up to the men to get what I wanted, be that something for my research or something as basic as a meat-free meal. One night, I stood watching the iftar line and noticed Brother Bill using the same spoon to scoop servings from a pan of chili mac and a pot of veggie beans. A strict vegetarian, I found it frustrating and mentioned it to Sister Nailah and her sister. The women told their mom, Aisha, who went up to the brothers to say something. Brother Naeem handed Bill a new spoon to use. Watching the scene unfold, I told Nailah that I needed to hide behind her in the line, because I knew Bill would be pissed at me. She laughed and said, "Yeah, he's gonna blame the white girl! The white girl said something!" I asked whether she would get me a plate, but Nailah said no. "Have we taught you *nothing*, Pam? Get up there and tell him you want it!" Her lesson underlined that you must stand up to brothers if you want to be a sister in *this* masjid community.

CHAPTER FIVE

"That's What They Think of Us"

I arrived at the masjid as believers were gathering for iftar on a late July evening in 2014. When the fasting women and men entered the property, they passed a large donation of goods heaped in a corner of the parking lot. Piles of trash bags stuffed with used clothes and household items had been stacked against the steps of the storage trailer. The bags seemed to have arrived earlier in the day from an unknown donor. Having observed a similar scene several times over the years, I expected believers to walk over and pick through the donation for what they wanted. But their comments quickly turned to anger, not curiosity or excitement.

"They need some place to dump it, so they dump it here," Brother Elijah started.

"Ain't that right?!" Brother Naeem replied. "This is the Goodwill."

"And we got nowhere to put it. Bins already full." Elijah managed garbage at the mosque, and his comment implied that he would throw the bags away. Later in the night, Sister Ava advised me not to take Elijah's words too literally, suggesting that he would pick through the bags for what he wanted before disposing of the rest. Even so, the frustration in his voice captured a palpable tension that night.

"That's disrespectful," added Sister Dina. "That's what they think of us. We need to stop accepting that stuff. That's not who we are."

No one saw the dumping take place, but I knew "they" meant immigrant Muslims, likely one of the Arab or South Asian families who routinely dropped off donations during Ramadan. Further exacerbating the sense of "dumping" was that the giver did not stay to pray or break the fast, even though he or she probably had driven many miles in LA traffic to drop off the goods.

The MAQ community relied on the help of their Arab and South Asian religious brethren to fulfill charitable obligations during Ramadan and to help grow the mosque community, as we saw with the food giveaways in chapter 1 and donated dirt in chapter 2. Believers across class lines enjoyed receiving free clothing and household items, especially sisters on fixed incomes. They found it challenging to afford festive modest clothes for masjid celebrations, such as the colorful South Asian pantsuits known as *shalwar kameez* that women at MAQ wore for Eid.[1] Even Dina and Naeem, who were well off compared with many members, took donations left at the masjid by other Muslim communities to share with family and friends. In other words, it wasn't the donation itself so much as *how* it was offered that had offended believers that July evening. Piles of haphazardly stacked trash bags left in the parking lot reflected two assumptions undercutting believers' attempts to construct a sense of moral worth in the neighborhood. First was the assumption that people in the MAQ community needed charity so badly they would take anything; second, that believers had time for the hours of unplanned labor required to organize the goods for distribution. Therefore, the donation denied the community the ability to decide for itself what it needed or how it could best be helped. It reinforced believers' perceptions that their Muslim brothers and sisters from immigrant-led communities looked down on them, a sentiment captured best in Sister Dina's comment "That's what they think of us."

According to Mauss, a gift is never neutral.[2] It represents a set of expected social relations, and once given—indeed *because* it has been given—"it is this object and not another."[3] In the giving of religious gifts, believers communicate implicit and explicit messages about how they relate to one another and to God.[4] When acts of charity were done in consultation with MAQ leaders, the community experienced a greater sense of control over what was distributed and how, creating the perception of a partnership rather than a dependence. By contrast, the "dumping" on this July evening made MAQ look like a thrift store, shining a light on the community's poverty rather than its common piety. It constructed a hierarchy of power in which African American Muslims receive, while immigrant Muslims give.

Of the estimated 3 million to 7 million Muslims in the United States, the three largest subpopulations are South Asian (35 percent), Arab or Middle Eastern (25 percent), and African American (20 percent). The remaining 20 percent includes first- and second-generation immigrants from Africa and other parts of Asia as well as some Latino converts. In the words of Islamic studies scholar Jane Smith, "America today is home to the most heterogeneous Muslim community at any time or place in the history of the world."[5] Many experts point to this diversity as evidence for the potential of a colorblind *ummah* (community of all believers). However, as one legal scholar notes, "Muslim Americans are also disparately situated along economic lines."[6] Arab and South Asian Americans share similar socioeconomic characteristics that put them ahead of most African Americans in terms of median household incomes, occupational levels, and educational attainment.[7] Stratification within the American ummah has received far less attention than ethnic diversity, but economic differences contribute to a sense that the American Muslim ummah is more divided than the Islamic ideal. Furthermore, the intersection of class and race inequalities threatens the very notion of an inclusive "brotherhood." For this reason, Jamillah Karim argues that within American Islam, "racialized boundaries run not between Black and white but between African American and immigrant."[8]

At the same time, Muslim Americans of *all* racial and ethnic identifications are under increasing threat from public and state-led Islamophobia.[9] The number of hate crimes against Muslims living in the United States has risen steadily since 9/11, with the FBI reporting more anti-Muslim assaults in 2016 than 2001.[10] Rather than gain special protections under the law to ensure their security, however, Muslim Americans are more often the target of heightened surveillance programs that seek to monitor and control their movements. The 2016 presidential campaign made clear that Islamophobia has become an accepted political mobilization tactic, with then candidate Donald Trump calling for a "total and complete shutdown of Muslims entering the United States"—a proposal he implemented with some success after becoming president with the so-called Muslim ban. Republican rival Ted Cruz offered a similarly discriminatory proposal during the campaign, arguing for a federal policy to "empower law enforcement to patrol and secure Muslim neighborhoods before they become radicalized."[11] Unbeknownst to Cruz, though, "the FBI and several local law enforcement agencies had already implemented some version of this bigoted idea."[12] Even so, Cruz managed to convince 45 percent of Americans to agree with his proposal.[13] Public hatred of Muslims also manifests in organized protests against the construction of new mosques in various US cities.[14] For these reasons, scholars of American Islam argue that the category Muslim has become a stigmatized one.[15]

While scholarship on the racialization of Islam captures the hardening of ethnoreligious boundaries in the United States, it obscures that *within* American Islam, important class differences intersect with existing racial inequalities to create intrareligious cleavages. This chapter brings to light moments when race/ethnicity surfaced as a salient source of difference between African American and immigrant Muslims, and it reveals how believers at MAQ responded to perceptions their Muslim brothers and sisters from other ethnic categories looked down on the MAQ community. I start by examining the ideal of Islam as a religion without racial hierarchy and how believers at MAQ make sense of this ideal in relation to their Blackness. Then come the subtle and not-so-subtle daily reminders of their position at the bottom of America's hierarchies of place and race. I found that in tense moments, such as the discovery of the trash bags described above, MAQ members responded by framing Arab and South Asian Muslims as less authentically American and more prone to gender oppression than African American Muslims. Such ethnic cleavages stand in stark contrast to the ideal of an inclusive ummah, but they do not emerge in a vacuum. Muslims of different ethnic backgrounds learn to situate themselves against others precisely because they live at the intersection of America's racial and religious orders. While there is much Othering that happens among African American and immigrant Muslims, what tensions ultimately reveal is the enduring legacy of white supremacy in the United States and its cascading impacts on the everyday lives of US Muslims.

"Muslims Constitute One Brotherhood"

On the eve of my first Ramadan at MAQ, Imam Khalid distributed a photocopied printout of the Prophet Muhammad's last sermon. It read: "All mankind is from Adam and Eve. An Arab has no superiority over a non-Arab nor a non-Arab has any superiority over an Arab; also a white has no superiority over a black nor a black has any superiority over white except by piety and good action. Learn that every Muslim is a brother to every Muslim and that the Muslims constitute one brotherhood." Notice there is no claim here of an Islam without color or ethnicity, just that there is no hierarchy in Allah's eyes. Imam Khalid referred to the Prophet's sermon many times over the years, also offering the life and practices of the Prophet (the body of literature known as Sunnah) as proof that within Islam, all races are equal.

Believers clung to the ideal of Islam as a faith without racial privilege, telling me there are no pictures or images of the Prophet Muhammad, and therefore he cannot be identified as white, Arab, or Black. This is partly why cartoons of the Prophet—typically depicted in a robe and turban to signify stereotypes of Arab culture—offend so many Muslims around the world. Considered idolatry, a blasphemous act in Islam, such images destroy the ideal of a racially inclusive religious ummah. The cartoons and the vast public attention they receive also contribute to public perceptions that Islam is an Arab faith, a categorically inaccurate belief held by most Americans.[16]

For African American Muslims, there is another, more historically rooted problem with racialized portrayals of the Prophet. Brother Fareed Jr., son of the masjid treasurer, explained that portrayals of Jesus as white and idyllic have been used for centuries to justify the oppression of people of color in the United States.[17] Without an image of the Prophet Muhammad to idolize, in Fareed's words, there can be no one race that "holds it over another." In framing Islam as a faith that offers an alternative to Christianity, African American Muslims try to overcome what Carolyn Rouse calls the "emotional wounds" suffered from centuries of social, cultural, and scientific negation.[18]

Believers' words about the Prophet help them narrate a larger story about race in the United States: they may live in an American society in which African Americans have faced targeted historical oppression, but within Islam can be found hope for a future where all humans are equal, regardless of skin color. Imam Khalid taught that "people don't think what they thought twenty, fifteen, ten, five years ago. The world as we know it is in constant flux." He latched on to the notion that America is changing to offer racial hope. "Old races are dying out, and new races are being born. People are intermingling with people, creating new races . . . or I should say new ethnicities. The world is not Black and white. It never has been — that was just the racist way of thinking." Then Khalid drew from demographics to support his claim: "Scientists are telling us those called the majority today will be the minority, and those that will be in the majority will be people of color." Like scholars, Khalid saw the ummah as a harbinger of further change.

Yet despite the shared ideal of an inclusive American ummah, when coming together in religious spaces to worship, the Muslim American community is deeply segregated. Three-fourths of all mosques in the United States are dominated by one ethnic category.[19] In most cases, the dominant group is either South Asian, Arab, or African American. Of the mosques that are evenly mixed, the most common combination is Arab and South Asian, a combination that's not random. Many religious traditions teach tolerance and brotherly love, but they also exist within systems of racial categorization that place some categories squarely above others.[20] In the United States, this means there are direct incentives for immigrants to situate themselves within or next to privileged categories. This is why we see Arab Americans often selecting "white" as their race on surveys and why South Asian Americans readily admit to a preference for white neighborhoods and schools in interview studies.[21] This ethnic boundary making often results in explicit attempts by Muslim newcomers to seek social and physical distance from Black Americans. Muslim scholar Su'ad Abdul Khabeer explains, "Like all immigrants to the United States, Arab and South

Asian migrants are encouraged to adopt ideologies of anti-Blackness as an immigrant rite of passage. They are primed to see U.S. Black Americans as less-than and deviant—a pathological and downwardly mobile population that is best avoided."[22] Khabeer is careful to recognize that "the racial logics of white supremacy" also work against Arab and South Asian Americans; but she, like Sherman Jackson, concludes that immigrant Islam constitutes an "ethnoreligious hegemony" that directly undermines the religious authority and authenticity of African American Muslims despite the latter's longer history in the United States.[23] When combined with the ways that white supremacy incentivizes anti-Blackness, this ethnoreligious hegemony causes Blackness to be perceived as "un-Islamic" when combined with religion.[24]

"Tell Us Some Solutions*"*

Like most African American–led mosques, the membership of Masjid al-Quran was overwhelmingly Black. The Arab and South Asian men who attended jumah rarely stayed long enough afterward to participate in the marketplace, so believers assumed these men came to the masjid only because it was close to their workplace. Women of Arab and South Asian heritage were even less frequent attendees. However, there was one Arab man who was a regular presence at MAQ: Egypt-born Sheikh Burhan. He worked as a Muslim chaplain in a state prison outside Los Angeles and, at the invitation of Imam Khalid, served as a guest imam one Friday per month. He also led the Taraweeh prayers two to three nights per week during Ramadan.

Though the MAQ community respected the man's work in the prison, seeing prison ministry as an important service to the African American community at large, many members openly despised the sheikh's style of teaching. Burhan regularly spoke in khutbahs about the importance of treating women with respect as a core of Islam, but he openly criticized unwed mothers and families with "illegitimate children" while associating these tropes with South Central, home to most of the believers. At the same time, he tried to align himself with the Black community, boasting, "Oh, I'm African American. I've been with the African American community since, well, since I came to this country in [the 1970s]." He said this in front of a group of sisters I was hanging out with, right after asking them whether I was Black because I had been at MAQ for so long. I was aghast, and the women awkwardly laughed. Where the conversation went next shows exactly why so many sisters disliked the sheikh.

In front of the sisters, Burhan asks where my child is when I'm at MAQ. I tell him, "With her dad, at home."

"Are you married yet?"

"No."

Burhan sighs and says I should be. Then he launches into a speech about my daughter's father having rights and how we should be married. This isn't the first time that Burhan has scolded me for having a child outside marriage. Still, I find myself furious tonight at the brazen way he does this in front of the sisters. I try to end the conversation, saying, "I know how you feel."

"No, you cannot know how I feel," he rebuffs. "Only Allah can know."

I move away, but the inquisition follows. Sister Aisha comes over and sits down next to me. With Burhan still going on, she leans in and whispers in my ear, "He's still gonna be her daddy, whether you're married or not. Does she know [you're not married]? No. Being married doesn't change who her daddy is." Then she gives Burhan a sharp look. He says he won't talk about it again and leaves our area. Aisha tells me her husband didn't want to come to MAQ tonight because Burhan was leading Taraweeh.

Here I am, a woman of privilege who doesn't wish to be married, and I'm being publicly branded by Burhan as a moral failure. Whether he realizes it or not, his critique of me puts women at MAQ in an untenable position. Like other imams who taught there, he attaches women's piety to motherhood but then makes that role legitimate only in marriage. His verbal lashing in front of sisters who want to be married but can't find husbands who provide in the ways they hope for (discussed in chapter 4) was insulting. Their small acts of resistance, avoiding MAQ when Burhan taught or waiting outside during his khutbahs, furthered their sense of community solidarity against racial outsiders.

*　　*　　*

One of the reasons Burhan felt he had license to publicly criticize me is that earlier in my fieldwork, we had struck up a friendship outside MAQ. I visited him at the prison, where all the Muslim inmates he worked with were African American. On one of my visits, I participated in a belated Eid celebration with men from one the cellblocks. It had taken Burhan months to get approval for the special dinner, an annual tradition he said was becoming more difficult because of political pressures on the warden. We shared dinner on communal tables inside an empty dining hall between regular mealtimes. The food was still prison food—heavy on starches, light on flavor—but the occasion felt festive because of the special treatment that allowed the men to eat together in peace, away from other inmates. The men shared stories of fasting and of the importance of being Muslim as a means of self-protection. As Burhan later explained in his office, gangs control the inside of the prison, and the men I met would have had no choice but to be in a Black-led gang—*except* that being identified as Muslim granted them license to opt out. Burhan said the gangs respect what Islam has done for African Americans, with Malcolm X continuing to serve as the model of counterinsurgency in many Black communities. He explained that the men "want to divorce their previous lives," which is why they come to Islam in prison. "It's a chance to start anew."

Burhan was protective of the men in a fatherly way while also critical of their choices. He shared that one of the men I spent the most time talking with during the Eid meal had killed his sister's rapist. Burhan wanted me to get the point that the mild-mannered man with round spectacles had few choices and was to be respected for protecting the honor of a woman. However, when the sheikh shared stories like this at MAQ, whether during iftar or, worse, during a khutbah, his words conflated the space of the prison with the masjid. Believers took offense at the portrayal of the inmates' problems as their own, because it violated their efforts to separate the moral order of the Muslim community from that of the neighborhood.

Burhan lived a life of modest means, believing his work in the prison was more important than making money. I respected the effort he put into counseling the men, including meditation circles and interfaith initiatives. Nonetheless, his experiences in the prison skewed his perceptions of African American communities as a whole. He emphasized youth violence and sexual abuse on several occasions. Often, he referred to the men who had grown up in South Central as those who had lived in the worst conditions, talking openly about these conditions when trying to encourage the MAQ community through Islam. Because of the segregation among mosques in the United States, experiences with Burhan were disproportionately important for MAQ members. He was one of their main points of contact with the immigrant Muslim community, and thus his perspective on South Central influenced how believers understood the ways the outside world perceived them.

Unfortunately, Burhan is not alone in misunderstanding the lives of believers in South Central. I attended a small number of fund-raisers and events at other Islamic centers over the years, and in these moments away from MAQ had the opportunity to question Muslims from other communities about their perceptions of problems within the ummah. At one event, I talked with a community health worker who told me her organization— a clinic built by Muslim physicians—did not engage in much outreach with the African American–led mosques in South Central. She described the problems of African American communities as "different," attributing the differences mainly to poverty. For example, she said that organizing a book fair doesn't work, because people in the area often lack "even six dollars for a book." They may be single with kids and thus "can't spend" money in that fashion. The South Asian sister expressed gratitude that she didn't have to live in South Central, singling out a recent police raid on a crack house near the clinic and the abundance of fast-food restaurants as evidence that its residents live in undesirable conditions. Her views of South Central paralleled the stereotypes many Angelenos hold about the area, which they perceive as full of gangs, drugs, and broken families.[25] Such views were based not on experience but on tropes. Had the woman attended jumah at MAQ, she would have seen books for sale and plenty of other goods that cost over six dollars.

Believers at MAQ recognize that African Americans face higher rates of poverty and its related social problems, discussing them in private with one another and with me, but they didn't want to be reminded of these problems by racial outsiders and especially not by fellow Muslims. The same night that Aisha came to my rescue at Burhan's inquisition, Sister Khadijah pulled me aside, livid about the sheikh. She had stormed out of the prayer hall while Burhan was giving his minilessons between *rakats* (units of prayer). Khadijah mimicked Burhan, "'You have the highest rate of teenage pregnancy. You have the highest rate of [incarceration]'?" She shouted, "We know that!" Later, in a calmer tone, she added, "Tell us some *solutions*. We already know all that." Khadijah was pleading for her Muslim brother from Egypt to stop judging African Americans based on trenchant stereotypes and to start helping them.

"What Do They Think? We Just Came to the Religion Yesterday?"

Every year, a handful of members had the privilege of traveling abroad to go on hajj, the holy pilgrimage that's one of the five pillars of Islam and an obligation for any able-bodied Muslim having the financial means to carry out at least once in his or her lifetime. Often, those who went were middle-class professionals who had saved for years to afford the expensive journey. Others, including Sister Ava, could go when wealthier Muslims sponsored them. Because so few in the MAQ community go on hajj, those who did received special attention with a community dinner to honor them upon their return. They also earned the title of Hajjah or Hajji (for women and men, respectively) to distinguish them from other members, with this special salutation added to their name when it appeared in programs for community events or in obituaries. Altogether, hajj represented a tremendous honor that generated respect and authority.

Hajj also represented a moment of profound hope for all believers. In his autobiography, Malcolm X described with jubilation his experience walking side by side with men of all skin colors while on hajj. He took from his time in Mecca a belief that Islam was the answer to racism: "America needs to understand Islam, because this is the one religion that erases from its society the race problem. Throughout my travels in the Muslim world, I have met, talked to, and even eaten with people who in America would have been considered white—but the white attitude was removed from their minds by the religion of Islam. *I have never before seen sincere and true brotherhood practiced by all colors together,* irrespective of their color."[26] However, for believers at MAQ fortunate enough to make the holy pilgrimage, hajj was rarely the racial utopia they hoped for. They recounted stories of discrimination and segregation while on the sacred journey. Sister Mira made hajj in 2007 and told me that Africans are treated the worst when trying to get into certain sacred spaces, such as the Prophet's tomb. Her group, led by an African American tour guide, tried its best to blend in with Indonesian women.

The neighborhood and its negative public reputation also shadowed believers while in Mecca. Sisters Ava and Aisha went on hajj together in 1993 and recalled watching Saudi television replay images of LAPD officers assaulting Rodney King in 1991 as well as of the uprising that followed the officers' acquittals in 1992. The women were more than eight thousand miles from home yet unable to escape their neighborhood's tattered public image, with global media coverage using a "crime frame" that perpetuated negative images of Black Americans and Black urban spaces like South Central.[27] Through a process that Loïc Wacquant famously calls "territorial stigmatization," residents of poor urban neighborhoods become symbolically attached to the negative conditions around them.[28] "Whether or not these areas are in fact dilapidated and dangerous . . . matters little in the end: when it becomes widely shared and diffused, the prejudicial belief that they are suffices to set off socially noxious consequences," Wacquant writes.[29] Prejudices toward residents of stigmatized areas affect the texture of everyday interactions. We see this clearly in how Ava and Aisha couldn't escape the images of South Central as a crime-saturated area despite being halfway around the world in Saudi Arabia. Even in privileged moments abroad, away from the national system of racial formation in the United States, African American Muslims find themselves facing racial discrimination and stereotyping.[30]

Contributing to these layers of ethnic tension were believers' feelings that immigrant Muslims look down on their African American sisters and brothers for having a limited knowledge of the Arabic language, a difference reinforced by the MAQ community's need to import native Arabic speakers like Burhan during Ramadan.[31] Believers also expressed frustration about immigrants assuming that African Americans know less about the religion as a result of their history as "converts." Said one sister, "I'm tired of it. . . . What do they think? We just came to the religion yesterday?" She expressed a common sentiment within the community that African Americans are made to feel like novices in Islam by people from Muslim-majority countries, saying that immigrants want to police members' dress and correct their stances during salat. I observed the latter happening once when Burhan's wife, a Moroccan woman, entered the prayer line late and, just before prayer, interrupted the calm to tell a line of young women they should stand a certain way. All these women were second-generation Muslims who had grown up practicing Islam.

From believers' perspectives, African Americans share a set of historical experiences, including a legacy of slavery, forced segregation, and repeated racial discrimination, that distinguish their religious trajectories. Imam Saleem said one Friday, "Many of us came from the auction block to the 'hood block!" This history informed their religious authority, which they often saw being illegitimated in the ummah rather than respected. Consequently, Imam Khalid, though hopeful about the future of US demographics, emphasized the community's successes in the Nation of Islam in his public lectures at other mosques. He wanted non-Black Muslim audiences to understand that African Americans are agentic people capable of accomplishment on their own terms.

"That's Their Culture!"

Throughout its history in the United States, Islam has stood as a symbol of racial resistance in African American communities. This is what drew thousands of Black Americans into Islam in the 1950s and 1960s, and its promise of self-determination helped influence the Civil Rights movement.[32] And it was precisely because of the political efforts of African Americans across faiths that the climate in the United States changed in the mid-1960s to allow nonwhite immigrants.[33] Believers thus rightly interpret the formation of "new races" in the United States as a direct result of Black America's political struggles in its own fight for greater inclusion. But rather than experiencing immigrant communities' gratitude for the Civil Rights movement and its impact on immigration reform, African American Muslims have become among the most marginalized within the ummah. According to Jamillah Karim, South Asian immigrants have done little to reject their privileged minority status, instead accepting the unspoken distinction between themselves and African Americans.[34] In her book *American Muslim Women* (2008), she argues that African American Muslims understand that this distinction comes at their direct expense. The result, unfortunately, is heightened ethnic tension between Muslims that, while not constant, becomes experienced situationally as discrimination and Othering by both sides.

A conversation I had with Sister Khadijah captures this well. She briefly attended the "big King Fahd" mosque, a lavishly adorned Islamic center in Culver City, in part to get away from the financial squabbling at MAQ and to enjoy the diversity of Islam in the United States. She stopped attending, however, after some of the sisters there pulled her aside to say she needed to have her ankles covered. After showing me where her skirt had hit, about three inches above the ankles, she exclaimed, "How you gonna tell me what to do?! In *my* country?" Khadijah's words point to a strongly felt tension among believers at MAQ that immigrant Muslims try to impose their religious authority on their African American counterparts. Members often drew from their nationality—in other words, *we* are Americans—as the frame to resist attacks on African Americans' knowledge and practice of Islam. This isn't surprising when we consider how Muslims are often framed in public discourses as "foreign."[35] Members at MAQ are incentivized through this discourse to situate themselves as distinct from immigrant Muslims, much in the same way that newcomers to the United States find it advantageous to situate themselves as distinct from African Americans.[36]

*   *   *

In the previous chapter, I showed how women at MAQ promoted a certain degree of patriarchy in hopes of advancing Black men while using traditional gender roles to try to liberate themselves from racial oppression. In earlier work, I also discussed how women in the MAQ community positioned their active mosque participation *in opposition* to that of immigrant Muslim women in order to resist controlling images of Muslim women as oppressed.[37] In both cases, women used gender as a frame to understand themselves vis-à-vis Muslims of other ethnic categories. A similar process of gendered boundary making occurred among brothers at MAQ. I was talking with Brother Naeem about my research one day, trying to explain why I felt comfortable at MAQ despite my status as a racial outsider. I told him that I had begun my field work while going to another mosque in LA but didn't feel as comfortable. He asked where I went, and I told him that I couldn't reveal the name for ethical reasons but that the mosque was mainly "immigrant or with Arab-run leadership." Right away Naeem said, "That's cuz they women haters. In Saudi Arabia too. You know? I never knew this, but Mira [his ex-wife] told me Saturday night how when we were in Saudi Arabia last year she was walking in the street, and this bus driver pushed into her with his bus [*uses hands to indicate the bus tapping her*]. She never told me that, probably cuz I would have hit him." Naeem's declaration that Arabs are "women haters," while undoubtedly stigmatizing, served a larger purpose. He wanted to differentiate American Muslims from foreign ones, whom he sees as more likely to have their understandings of Islam corrupted by cultural traditions around gender. He did not see Islam as inherently flawed, more that pure Islam wasn't being practiced when women went unprotected.[38] In framing Muslims from other countries as gender oppressors, Naeem asserted his right to use an American identity as a source of authority, which, although African Americans are discriminated against in the United States, offers greater basic liberties to women than some Muslim-majority countries.

Putting this in conversation with Khadijah's comment that the United States is "her" country, members clearly used a nativist lens in their efforts to exert American superiority.[39] Even Sister Ava, the community's most vocal advocate for interethnic harmony, phoned me fuming one day about a fellow sister and friend who was "all covered up now," with nothing but her face showing. Ava shouted angrily, "That's not Muslim!" After a pause, she more slowly but still animatedly added, "That's their *culture!*" The change in dress came after the sister went on hajj with a group of immigrant Muslims, violating the norm of traveling in an African American–led tour. It was this same folk separation of "culture" and "religion" that Imam Khalid drew from to rally the community not to give up hope after Imam W.D. Mohammed's death in 2008. Khalid told believers, "We have our own food, our own clothing. We don't want to give ourselves in to what they want." Then he said, "We like how we look. . . . You can't escape you and how you look. You can have on—What's that thing? A burqa?—but that's not Islam!"

∗   ∗   ∗

Despite Muslims' desires to frame Islam as a tool for racial equality, hierarchies of race and place affect how believers of different ethnic backgrounds understand one another. The limited numbers of immigrant Muslims who visited MAQ tended to look through a class-based frame, singling out poverty as a distinguishing characteristic of African American Muslim communities. Given that ample demographic research demonstrates that South Asian and Arab Americans earn more than African Americans and attain more education, the frame goes beyond being one of difference within Islam to one that reinforces existing social inequalities in the larger American society. Believers at MAQ responded with their own frame, separating the practices of certain Muslims from the faith so as to position African Americans as distinctly American authorities on Islam. Given that their non-Muslim family members tend to focus on women's treatment in the mosque as the main fault of Islam, which we saw in discussions of "His-lam" in chapter 4, it's not surprising they used gender as a frame to fight back against their racial marginalization. Identification is situational and contingent, forming an ongoing process of being summoned and summoning in relation to others.[40] Believers will feel their Muslimness with family and other African Americans, but in their interactions in the ummah, they're more likely to feel both their Blackness and their lower socioeconomic status.

Being Black in South Central intersects with being Muslim in America, creating a feeling of acute difference through which believers must negotiate intersecting identifications. In their efforts to correct misconceptions about Islam as part of "their culture," believers perpetuated stereotypes of certain Muslims as foreign, reinforcing differences rather than uniting all believers under the ideal of the ummah. At the same time, the masjid needed immigrants to financially support the organization. This put members in an awkward position of having to recognize their hardship enough to warrant charitable aid but not enough to discount their moral worth. How they did this is the focus of the next section.

"We Did Not Have Any Money"

On a partly cloudy Saturday in 2009, believers gathered in the parking lot of nearby Excellence in Learning Charter School to celebrate its dedication. Under an expansive rented tent, three dozen members of Masjid al-Quran sat in their Friday best on several rows of rented folding chairs. They watched quietly as Imam Khalid unveiled a plaque honoring the people responsible for funding the K–5 school. Of the twelve names of individuals and organizations listed on the plaque as "major contributors," half were from overseas, including two foundations. Two more names of organizations were ambiguous and could have been from outside the United States (e.g., Muslim Businessmen and Women). Of the four individual contributors listed, two were African American, but only one of those was a regular MAQ member (Sister Haleema); the other was a famous Muslim athlete not present at the ceremony. The MAQ community was listed last, after the nonprofit that Imam Khalid and his wife had created to operate the school.

Recall from chapter 2 that the MAQ community had bought the current property in 1973 when the parcel included a brick building large enough to house a Nation of Islam temple and a Clara Muhammad school. Earthquake damage made the structure unsafe, and MAQ had to tear it down. "We did not have any money at the time," Khalid told the crowd, "but we had hope and faith." MAQ's hope was to build a school on the property as the first step in a three-phase construction plan. Now, more than twenty years later, its leaders could boast that phase 1 was complete, though the school had originally been planned as a private Islamic school.

Khalid thanked the donors who helped make the construction of the school possible, mentioning amounts of $600K, $295K, and $230K from Saudi men and women. He introduced and thanked two South Asian donors, who each spoke for several minutes. Then he explained that the community had borrowed another $200K from an immigrant-led mosque outside Los Angeles and received funding for twenty-five computers from the African American Muslim athlete. Then Khalid said, "Beside every good man is a good woman." He announced that Sister Haleema sold one of her rental houses to give the masjid the additional $85K needed to complete construction.

The event was joyous, with big smiles on the faces of everyone who participated. Brother Naeem's Cheshire grin is front and center in many of the pictures I took that day. However, given that hundreds of MAQ's members had contributed throughout the twenty-year construction project, the number who showed up to celebrate the school's dedication was rather paltry. Attendance was low because by that point, many believers had lost their enthusiasm for the school. The reasons shed new light on how believers at MAQ relate to the larger communities in which their mosque is embedded. First, the long-awaited school was no longer the Islamic one promised as a replacement for the revered Sister Clara Muhammad School. Alumni of that school, who make up a significant proportion of the middle-aged members considered "young" at MAQ, thought they'd be able to send their own children to a reincarnation of their alma mater. According to school officials, though, not enough of these Muslim families could afford a private school tuition. Nor were there enough Muslims from immigrant-led communities willing to drive their children into the inner city to attend.

Had it been able to then become a charter school that was not Muslim but still majority Black, Excellence in Learning (EIL) might have remained a beacon of hope for the community nonetheless. Again, believers say that this is what leaders had promised. But in the time it took to build the school, a drastic change occurred in the MAQ neighborhood's demographics. South Central became home to waves of new migrants from Mexico and Central America. Children who filled the inaugural K–5 cohorts at EIL were overwhelmingly from Latino families (nearly 90 percent of households around the mosque identify as Hispanic or Latino). The handful of Black families from MAQ who enrolled later took their children out, finding EIL to be an unwelcoming space. Many believers no longer identified the school as anything more than a way for MAQ to collect revenues. Of course, given the lack of transparency that obfuscates financial dealings in the mosque community, most of the women and men I talked with about EIL doubted that the rent income was actually going to their community. The school may represent the crown jewel of believers' collective efforts over the past two decades and their greatest contribution to the neighborhood since the 1970s, but in this moment of celebration the community could not escape its new reality as a Black urban religious island.

Nor could the community hide from its dependence on Muslim immigrants. The only MAQ member to receive individual recognition that day had to sell one of her properties to come up with the needed money to complete phase 1 of the project, and even then the amount she donated paled in comparison with the funds donated by Arab and South Asian Muslim outsiders. Members' lower socioeconomic positioning relative to other Muslim communities was unavoidable thanks to Imam Khalid's rare public accounting of the mosque's actual cash position. And it didn't pass unnoticed that while immigrant Muslims would donate money to build a school, they had no interest in sending their own children there.

Now the school serves pork-eating Christian Latino children—at least that's how believers talked about it. They discussed the need to protect the Muslimness of the space by keeping haram products off the campus, but there was only so much the school could do. For the brothers who once worked as Fruit of Islam soldiers policing the streets of South Central, it was an affront to their dignity to drive past a vendor selling pork rinds at the school gate as they entered the MAQ grounds for Friday community prayers. The crowds of students and their parents who clustered around that cart exceeded the handful of believers shopping at the masjid market after jumah. The school had become an unwanted mirror of truth, reflecting the community's struggles to survive amid a changing social landscape in South Central—simultaneously a reminder of religious differences with their neighbors and economic differences with their Muslim brethren. For these reasons, believers often rejected the narrative of pride in EIL that leaders tried to promote, reinforcing internal fissures.

"You Don't Know My Situation!"

The MAQ community's dependence on immigrant Muslims for financial support had yet another unintended consequence, one that created conflict among believers along class lines. The Eid al-Fitr festival celebrating the end of Ramadan was the busiest day of the year at the mosque, with hundreds of African American Muslims joining festivities, including believers from other parts of the city. According to Sister Mira, compared with immigrant Muslims, who want to "pray, eat, and leave," African American Muslims "make a day of it," with inflatable bouncy houses for the kids and live music. For those who lingered late into the day, there may even be dancing, which could be considered haram in other spaces.[41] The festival also signaled a time of charitable giving, with the imam's wife, Sister Dina, organizing toy drives and other giveaways at MAQ.

In contrast to the anger she expressed over the dropped-off trash bags of donations in the opening vignette, at Eid al-Fitr in 2009 Sister Dina gratefully received a large donation of toys from an immigrant-led Muslim community. The toys were all given out within minutes, demonstrating a strong desire from the families for these charitable gifts. This donation differed from the trash bags in two key ways: the toys were brand new, not the unwanted goods of other Muslims; and they were given to Dina in advance, allowing her time to organize how best to distribute them. But charity is never a neutral act, and "gifts" from immigrant Muslim communities, when redistributed by masjid leaders, tended to expose internal class hierarchies. I volunteered during several giveaways, following Dina's instructions on how to pass out goods. Then I would hang out in the evening at the tables with the believers who had acquired the donations. They expressed frustration about how middle-class members like Dina controlled access to resources, dictating who received what. In addition, they felt that the community's wealthy held their class status over others.

An intense interaction between Sisters Ava and Dina—friends for decades—illustrates these issues well. After a giveaway, Dina accused Ava of taking goods she didn't need, telling her, "You're not poor."

Ava was livid. She shot back, "You don't know my situation! I'm on a fixed income. What I got to do, show you my checks?"

The heated exchange drove Ava to tears—tears that were a mixture of hurt feelings and anger at her wealthier African American Muslim sister. She was frustrated that Dina tried to control what she received. She told me later that she shared the goods she picked up at MAQ with her Latino neighbors, including an undocumented family who lived next door. She saw this redistribution as part of her own obligation to perform zakat, helping others she perceived as less fortunate than she was. It was a way of deepening her din, incorporating personal hardship into pious social action. In Ava's eyes, Dina was trying to strip her of this moral agency while also judging her as less virtuous. She responded to Dina's judgment with accusations of greed and impropriety, saying she knew that many immigrant Muslims gave special monetary gifts to Imam Khalid and his wife during Ramadan.

She thought it was shady that these donations didn't get included in the mosque's accounting systems. Ava then pointed to Dina's luxury vehicles and flashy jewelry as proof that the imam's wife was implicated in her husband's alleged corruption.

*　*　*

In Iddo Tavory's study of an Orthodox Jewish community, the poorest members were those who devoted their lives to studying the Torah.[42] They gained special status within the Orthodox community for choosing spiritual devotion over material comfort. The poor at MAQ had no such choice. Their poverty was structurally imposed, and no matter how hard they tried to pull themselves up, there was always something pushing them back down. Not everyone at MAQ was poor, however, and even those who were experienced different needs and pious desires. Donors demonstrated a failure to recognize this variation within the African American Muslim community when they "dumped" goods at the masjid, offending believers who did not perceive themselves as needy (or needy enough for cast-off goods). Even those who donated goods in consultation with Sister Dina or her husband were unlikely to understand the intense suspicion and distrust that many believers felt about masjid leadership. In their acts of generosity, outsiders unintentionally exposed internal systems of inequality at MAQ in which those at the bottom of the class hierarchy assumed that those in positions of power did not distribute donated goods in a just manner.

Either case—blind charity or charity in partnership—reinforced to believers that their location in South Central made them categorically worse off than their Muslim brothers and sisters from wealthier communities. Blind charity appeared as pity, feeding existing hierarchies of power; charity in partnership, in which mosque leaders could control who received what, minimized feelings of marginality but fed theories of suspicion and distrust. Moreover, there's no official category distinguishing the pious poor from the nonbelieving poor, even if in public discourses we have some conceptions of "deserving" and "undeserving." So when immigrant Muslims conflated African American Muslims *in* a poor neighborhood with the problems *of* the neighborhood, it violated the moral distinction believers struggled so hard to create. Believers responded in ways that both hardened ethnic boundaries and offered opportunities to cultivate self-respect in a complicated urban landscape. The fact that they didn't make disparaging comments about Mormons, who also donated goods requiring extensive labor to distribute, supports my argument that it's because immigrant Muslims and African American Muslims share a religious identity—a religion

believers hoped could bring racial equality—that feelings of difference intensified and interethnic tensions were perpetuated. The reproduction of
ethnoreligious distinctions can change the very nature of religious experience, transforming religion into a mechanism of social inequality.[43]

"We Love Our Brothers.... But..."

Time and time again, charity was the interactional mechanism for feelings
of difference with outsiders. Recall that earlier in the book, I examined
the struggles believers faced trying to fulfill their charitable intentions in
a setting where people with drug and alcohol additions wander onto the
mosque property. They constructed a hierarchy of worth that was in direct
opposition to the perceived moral worth of others in the neighborhood, in-
vesting considerable labor in their efforts to construct symbolic boundaries
during their fulfillment of feeding the less fortunate. Charity in that earlier
case served as a means of deepening piety and moral superiority, whereas
charity in this case served as a reminder that within the ummah, MAQ is
seen as no different from its neighborhood. When members see trash bags
of donations on their property, they interpret the "gifts" as clear evidence
that their Muslim brothers and sisters of other ethnic backgrounds look
down on African Americans, violating believers' conceptions of self-worth.
If the core goal of MAQ members' strivings is to deepen their piety through
poverty, not against it, then it makes sense that they feel frustrated within
the ummah by the steady reminders of the community's stagnant socioeconomic status. What does it say to women and men at MAQ if they're always
the receivers in the ummah, regarded as lacking even six dollars for a book?

If anything, in moments of receiving charity from outsiders, believers
reaffirmed race as a primary identity marker, expressing unequivocally
their shared desire to keep MAQ an African American–led community.
Brother Louis articulated this well when he said in a khutbah, "No Arabs,
no Pakistanis. We don't want them as our head. We love our brothers, we
love 'em. But they've not been through what we been through, having
everything taken from us." His words point at the larger (white) US society that has capitalized on Black oppression to accumulate social, political, and economic advantages. Members of MAQ thus feel a need to protect their masjid as a safe space, even if it means rejecting greater inclusion
with non-Black Muslims. Remember that believers draw specifically from
the Prophet Muhammad's last sermon to explain race within Islam, which
recognizes that there are different races. This is how believers can remain
members of both the ummah and the larger African American community
without the two identifications being in conflict.

Religious congregations are the most ubiquitous kind of institution in the United States, and within these spaces participants "generate, sustain, remake, or eliminate racial identity and meaning."[44] This makes congregations fundamental to processes of racial formation and exclusion.[45] When differences within a religious community align with structural inequalities in US society, that community may reinforce and even perpetuate disadvantages. Such is what we see when members of MAQ feel they are looked down on by South Asian and Arab American Muslims and fight back with disparaging remarks about other Muslims that deepen divides within the American ummah rather than bridge them.[46] This experience undermines but does not erase the ideal of Islam as a religion of racial equality.

Believers undeniably felt more comfortable in majority-Black spaces, even when others in those spaces weren't Muslim. Imam Khalid said in a public lecture one year, "This is where we feel most comfortable, in communities populated by African Americans. African Americans don't believe all the things being said about the Muslims. What they say doesn't make us nervous, because we know [what] our friends, family, acquaintances think about us." As Khalid's words make clear, African American believers resist racial oppression by aligning themselves with other African Americans. This helps explain why the majority of African American Muslims choose to worship in African American–led mosques. Race constituted the lens through which believers perceived themselves and felt perceived by others.

At the same time, believers recognized that Arab and South Asian Americans face greater unjust scrutiny since 9/11. They sympathized with the struggles of immigrant women who wish to wear hijab and of people traveling through the airport with a Muslim name. There was a sense among believers at MAQ that after 9/11, immigrant Muslims could finally start to understand the kind of discrimination that African American Muslims have been experiencing their entire lives. After the attacks on the twin towers of the World Trade Center, when religion became a more salient social boundary for all Muslims in the United States, there was a moment of potential change within the ummah. Muslims of diverse ethnic backgrounds came together to fight stereotypes and protest violence both against and by Muslims, but this fellowshipping among America's diverse Muslim communities was not something I observed very often. What fellowshipping I observed tended to include MAQ organizing with other Black-led mosques. I think it would be inappropriate to call the charity efforts of other ethnic Muslim communities toward MAQ fellowshipping, because it was too often perceived as a sleight of hand to constitute a form of boundary crossing.

By giving to MAQ but not joining the community, Muslim outsiders signal that they are interested in a specific hierarchical relationship. Wrapping up the goods in trash bags says you/African Americans are in our/immigrant Islam, obligating believers at MAQ to accept a place in the ummah based on class rather than piety. The fact that much of the data for this chapter come from my fieldwork during Ramadan, the main time of the year in which other Muslims visited MAQ to fulfill their charitable obligations, reinforces that there is a particular kind of relationship being asked of African American Muslims. Implicit and explicit messages of hierarchy intensify members' frustrations at a time they also are trying to fulfill religious obligations to help the less fortunate. Admittedly, there is much more going on in these interactions from the perspectives of immigrant Muslims than what I have discussed, but I limit my arguments to what my data can speak to. What I offer is an interactional, on-the-ground perspective of a community of African American Muslims living and worshipping in a poor urban neighborhood. And in taking account of their perceptions and actions, this chapter shows in microlevel detail *how* religion "helps to create racially distinctive networks and, in using them as the basis for congregational and denominational growth, helps maintain and justify them."[47]

"Allahu Akbar"

Sister Ava often caught up on phone calls to loved ones while baking cakes in her kitchen. On a Saturday night in late May 2016, it was two lemon cakes for a family friend and longtime customer. At 8:42 p.m. PST, she phoned me in Texas. I was already asleep, albeit fitfully. The thunderstorms that were bombarding the South that spring woke me several times. I gave up on sleep just before six o'clock that morning and turned to my muted phone. I had a missed call and a voice mail from Ava, plus another missed call from an LA number I didn't recognize. I listened to Ava's message first:

> *Pamaloo, this is Mom. Checkin' on you* [pause] *and uh* [pause] *the water back there. Give me a text or a call and let me know you're alright.*

I smiled, thinking that Ava worried too much about me. I pictured her watching TV in her kitchen and, seeing news about flooding in Texas before grabbing the phone with her flour-covered hands. I turned to the other call, received at 12:03 a.m.:

> *Pam, this is Boo* [Ava's sister]. [Cries] *Pam, Ava passed away. Um. She passed away, Pam.*

"But Ava just called," I explained to a silent phone. Then a shattering mix of fear and sorrow took hold of me. My legs gave out. My daughter, four years old at the time, thought I was hurt and started to scream. Frantically, I phoned Ava's number, then her sister's, but got no response from either. Then I texted Ava's daughter-in-law, who called me right away. It was true, she said. Ava was gone. She had had a heart attack at home, in the middle of baking a cake. We cried together on the phone, both expressing the shock that would characterize everyone's reaction in coming days. Ava seemed healthy, all things considered. She had been taking medication for high blood pressure and had glaucoma in one eye, but you'd never know she suffered from either disease by the way she continued to push nonstop at sixty-nine years old. I would later learn that the symptoms of cardiac distress are different in women, slowly breaking down the body until it's often too late to stop a major attack, which is why heart disease is called a silent killer of women.

∗   ∗   ∗

Less than twelve hours after receiving the call from Ava's sister, I was on a plane to Los Angeles. Upon landing, I headed straight to Ava's house. There I found family members huddled in the kitchen, the same kitchen that Ava had been baking in the night before. Latching on to Boo, both of us hungry for comfort, I listened to her firsthand account of how Ava had passed. With the cake batter churning in the electric mixer and eggs in hand ready to crack, Ava felt a deep pain in her chest. She was losing her breath. She started screaming to her siblings in the house for help. Boo ran downstairs to Ava's side, frantically calling 911. Ava told Boo she wasn't ready to go, repeating over and over, "Allahu Akbar, Allahu Akbar" (God is great, God is great). As the paramedics entered the house, Boo said that all the breath in Ava's body escaped, like a long, deep sigh. She also told me that her sister was clearly in pain but thankfully didn't suffer for very long. I may have been shocked at Ava's death, but I wasn't surprised to hear that her final words were expressions of faith.

When I boarded the plane, my contacts at the mosque had thought that the *janaza* (burial) would be two days later on Tuesday, in accordance with the Muslim tradition of quickly burying the dead. Imam Khalid explained to me that this is done so that we don't mourn too long. We must accept God's will, he said of death. As the often quoted sura says, "To Allah we belong, and to Him is our return." However, by the time I got off the plane, the service had been postponed until at least Thursday. For Ava's non-Muslim kin, it was way too soon to be holding a service. They wanted family members traveling from other states to be able to arrive in time for the service, and they themselves wanted additional time to plan a more elaborate service. It was the first of many reminders that week of how African American Muslims straddle two distinct racial-religious cultures within their families.

I spent the next several days serving as a liaison between Ava's Christian family and her Muslim kin at the mosque. Sister Dina asked me to oversee the obituary, knowing I was close with several relatives and already spending many long hours at the yellow house. I was grateful to have something to do to stay busy, but I was ill prepared for the effect that the retelling of a person's life can have on surviving kin—in this case, two kinds of kin (legal/blood and religious). Even which name to put on the burial service program became a source of conflict. To her legal family, she was Avaline, but to her religious family she was always Sister Ava. Some of her closest friends at Masjid al-Quran, including Aisha, thought Ava would have been embarrassed by the Muslim community hearing her called by her birth name. After much discussion, we went with Hajjah Ava, followed by both her maiden surname and her late husband's Muslim surname. On the headstone, her kids put Avaline.[1]

Then came a struggle over which photo to place on the program cover. I went through hundreds from Ava's personal collection as well as photo albums and loose photos owned by her adult children. It was hard to find a recent photo that captured Ava's spirit. She had been self-conscious about gaps in her smile from lost and broken teeth, so in photos she kept her mouth closed tight, hiding the smile that warmed so many hearts. She intended to get her teeth fixed, but she wouldn't accept financial assistance from anyone to do it. Her pride prevented her, she said. Her daughters told me to use the last photo taken of their mother, at a party two days before her death. Several of us disagreed, finding Ava's skin looking pale and her clothes too muted in that picture. Her MAQ sisters liked one I had taken a few years prior, a profile portrait of Ava with her head draped in a bright coral-and-pink scarf. It better captured the Hajji's bright spirit, they said. We wanted to do justice to our friend's vivid character but worried about offending her offspring. Our solution was to print two versions of the program, with equal copies of each. Like the resolution of the name dispute, it represented a compromise bridging two cultures.

The struggles over the name and photo, as well as efforts by Ava's family to delay the funeral, worried mosque members. What if there was drama the day of the janaza? How would that affect Ava's path to paradise? Over the years, I've heard stories of Christian family members refusing to consent to Muslim burial traditions.

In the end, there wasn't much drama at the gravesite or at the cleansing and shrouding ceremony the day before. Ava's children did not contest a Muslim burial, in part because Ava had talked with them about what she wanted.[2] Everyone in her family knew how devoted she was to Islam, and they came together peacefully on a Thursday morning at a cemetery in nearby Inglewood. I estimated that as many as five hundred people came to the gravesite, though it was difficult to count while among the crowd. I know for certain that I had printed three hundred obituaries, handing them out with another sister, and that they were gone within ten minutes. The crowd was so thick that I couldn't see Imam Khalid as he delivered his eulogy, but I heard him twice explain to the family that Ava did not use the name by which her family called her. She had introduced herself to him as "Sister Ava," Khalid said.

After the graveside burial service, the attendees split into two camps. One proceeded to the masjid, where the MAQ community had organized a repast with halal food and R&B music. The other went to Ava's family home for an invitation-only repast. These non-Muslim blood kin wanted to celebrate Avaline with their own food and drinks, including alcohol. Only a handful of them made an appearance at MAQ.

Most Muslims in the United States are from countries with large Muslim populations or families with several generations of Muslims. Most African American Muslims, by contrast, are either converts or children of converts. They don't have the privilege of being able to assume that their family members understand or respect their religion. This complicates home life for members of MAQ, who strive to live a Muslim way of life, believing that their faith provides a path toward righteousness and salvation. Like Ava, they may feel torn between conflicting loyalties or insulted by the failure of their blood kin to accept their religious beliefs and practices. I had sat with Ava on several occasions as she broke down in tears over the feeling that her siblings in the house cooked pork in their shared kitchen just to taunt her. It may seem to be a minor offense, but to someone for whom both faith and food were defining elements of daily life, she could interpret their actions in no other way than as a symbolic assault on her din. Indeed, much of this book has been an examination of the efforts of believers at Masjid al-Quran to live a Muslim way of life and how this life, despite its ideals, becomes experienced as difference when it intersects with America's existing hierarchies of religion, race, class, gender, and place.

"If There Ain't Fists Being Thrown, You Know You Ain't Family Yet"

Despite their best intentions to emphasize their common humanity with neighbors, family, and Muslims of other ethnic backgrounds, believers at MAQ repeatedly faced reminders of their marginalization as religious and racial minorities. They struggled because of the very inequities they strove to surpass within an Islamic framework. This was true throughout the year but especially during Ramadan, the holy month when believers strove the hardest to deepen their faith and their collective actions became most intense. The obstacles believers faced in trying to feed the less fortunate, including moral debates over whom to feed, produced palpable tensions that threatened to undermine the positive spirit of Ramadan. These tensions intensified when there was not enough food to feed everyone in line for iftar, with some members seeking to deepen their piety by feeding the neighborhood hungry before serving themselves. Others thought that feeding intoxicated neighbors was haram, regardless of whether there was enough food. Through this charity work, the neighborhood summoned believers in different ways, perpetuating frustrations over internal gender and class differences.[3] Still, members saw each other as kinfolk—their chosen Muslim family complete with all the emotional labor and drama a family brings. As one sister joked, "If there ain't fists being thrown, you know you ain't family yet."

Believers were further tested during Ramadan when wealthier Muslims tried to feed and clothe the members of MAQ, who in turn had to make sense of their marginalization within the American ummah. For believers, their path through the Nation of Islam was a source of pride, because in the movement they learned to love their Blackness. Imam Khalid described the growth of the Nation during that time as a "lily grow[ing] out of a swamp." Yet in their interactions with Muslims of other ethnicities, who tended to fare better in terms of educational attainment and occupational status, members of MAQ saw their history being treated as a liability to religious authority. They felt they had to fight back against misconceptions about their beliefs and practices within Sunni Islam. The limited degree of interaction they had with Muslims of other ethnicities meant that the few Arab and South Asian American Muslims who visited MAQ and displayed discriminatory attitudes toward African American Muslims had a disproportionate effect on believers' understandings of their position in the ummah.

Apart from their charity work during Ramadan, believers emphasized a different kind of hard work, focusing on economic self-sufficiency and uplift. Halal economic exchange went beyond a survival strategy; it provided a means to deepen piety by rising above the perceived moral fray of the neighborhood, where jobs were too few and the lure of "fast money" too great. But the networks of exchange at MAQ were closed, meaning the exchange was more a redistribution of existing limited resources than a method of generating new wealth within the community. This put believers into competition with one another and the organization itself, causing distrust that impacted the community's growth. Importantly, the few believers who left MAQ to attend other mosques did so because of frustrations over drama with money. Economic struggle had ripple effects on all dimensions of community life as well as in believers' homes, where women and men found it difficult to enact their desires for a traditional family structure.

Yet even when intentions went unfulfilled, whether these were their efforts to develop and support Muslim businesses or their efforts to earn blessings through zakat, the very act of striving within an Islamic framework provided a way for believers to strengthen their din. Their being mindful of the interactional dilemmas that arose while living a Muslim way of life in South Central set up a new way of thinking about piety whereby religious community making is a technique of cultivating the body social. It is a way of extending Mahmood's work on religious agency to show how engaging in social life *is* the ethical formation. This effort involves women and men in a shared moral project, making community participation a part of achieving God consciousness, such that even when it creates burdens—indeed *because* it creates burdens—community participation serves to deepen piety. We see this project lived out in the creative ways women respond to their frustrations that men in the community can't live up to the qualities of the ideal Muslim husband, such as providing financial security so that women can be freer to contribute to society as mothers and nurturers. The sisterhood network that women at MAQ formed in response to their less-than-desirable marriage options incorporated ways of meeting not only material needs but spiritual and emotional desires as well. As a result, the women were enabled to cultivate joyous memories of raising their children together in South Central, countering dominant stereotypes of the area and flipping the script on misconceptions of Black motherhood.

The commitment that believers demonstrated toward living a Muslim way of life in an urban space marked by disadvantage and stigma allows us to view struggles as forms of pious action, not obstacles to it. Indeed, Black placemaking was woven into the foundations of living Islam, and vice versa. Believers drew from their religious tradition to navigate local life, even when it caused more complications. A mix of nostalgia for the glories of past decades and deep longing for a better future has kept the MAQ community together and pushing forward. There may be few neighbors left who are sympathetic to recruitment messages, and fund-raising campaigns may take decades to materialize—but, as Imam Khalid said, the community's aim has been and will be to improve South Central, not move away from it.

∗   ∗   ∗

Islam may be the fastest-growing religion in the United States, but it appears that African American Muslims may not be holding on to their mosques or building new ones. Research on the number and ethnic composition of mosques is limited, but one well-cited report suggests that African American–led mosques declined between 2001 and 2011.[4] This occurred during a time when the total number of mosques in the United States increased by *74 percent*.[5] It's possible that more African American Muslims are choosing to worship in ethnically mixed mosques, making the need for ethnically separate spaces void, but for believers at MAQ this certainly was not the case. They rarely left MAQ for a community led by Muslims of other ethnic backgrounds. More often, they shifted their attendance to a different African American–led mosque, stopped attending a mosque, or passed away.

Surveys indicate that the percentage of US Muslims who identify as Black or African American also is down.[6] This latter trend is partly due to the increase in the foreign-born Muslim population, reducing the relative proportion of African American Muslims. However, in light of the decrease in African American–led mosques, there is concern among African American Muslims that they are losing their communities.[7] MAQ proved to be an unexpectedly strategic site for understanding this decline, as many of the preceding pages portray a community struggling to survive. This struggle stands in painful contrast to believers' hopes for Islam to be a solution to their social ills.

Why are African Americans struggling to hold on to their mosques when elsewhere in the United States Islam is growing? The answer lies in America's trenchant systems of urban and racial inequality, which together make the maintenance of a religious community harder for African American Muslims. The fact that believers at MAQ compete with one another for access to a bedroom or shower at the mosque points to the deep disadvantage that characterizes members' socioeconomic statuses. Race or neighborhood alone are not explanations, though. Zain Abdullah's ethnographic research on Muslims in Harlem suggests that African immigrants are embedded in an "ethnic safety net" that protects and possibly bolsters their socioeconomic statuses as compared to African Americans in the same neighborhood.[8] The multiple overlapping inequalities that MAQ members face make their experiences qualitatively distinct, as the cumulative disadvantage of decades of living in South Central interacts with the historical oppression of race, class, and gender in the United States.

"This Was His Life"

With many believers now in their sixties and seventies, death seems imminent to members of this Muslim community. Ask a brother how he's doing, and he'll probably mention his gratefulness to Allah for being alive. Members bury their Muslim brothers and sisters regularly enough that mourning has become a routine part of community life. Since I left LA in 2015, several key figures at MAQ have returned to Allah: Brother Kareem, Brother Sulayman, Brother Fareed, Sister Haleemah, and of course Sister Ava. This is in addition to the members lost in the eight years prior. Their funerals have given the remaining members opportunities to process the many kinds of loss that have defined MAQ's history. Religion is built through such rituals, bringing people together and allowing them to experience similar thoughts or feelings.[9] Funerals thus represent deeply sacred moments for the living, full of reflection and gratitude.

I happened to have been on a plane headed to Los Angeles when Brother Fareed died. Within a few hours of landing, I received a call from Ava with the news. She had warned me four months earlier that Fareed was sick with prostate cancer. During Ramadan of that year, he was supposed to make breakfast for believers after the annual Night of Power prayers, but he went into the hospital instead. As Ava explained it, she and Aisha hopped in the car at the last minute, bought eggs, and served them with grits just in time. She may not have trusted Fareed with her money, but she loved her Muslim brother and didn't want to let him or the community down. While smaller than Ava's janaza, there were still over two hundred people at the gravesite to honor Fareed, most of them Muslims from MAQ or other mosques in Los Angeles. According to Imam Khalid, a larger, wealthier Islamic center donated the plot, and MAQ paid for the shrouding, burial, and repast. Sister Dina told me, "We owed him that. This was his life."

The MAQ community has spent tens of thousands of dollars to pay the burial costs of key members or to help organize memorials. I've come to realize through its organization of these funerals how exceptional MAQ is with its strong ties and its dedicated members willing to devote their time, money, and emotional energy to building a community in South Central. Take the example of Sister Sherri.[10] When she was lucid, Sherri displayed a sharp wit. She carried homemade cloth bags emblazoned with cutouts of then presidential candidate Barack Obama, and she loved to talk about politics. But Sherri was burdened by severe mental health problems, suffering from both substance abuse and uncontrollable outbursts. According to community folklore, she once famously stripped off her clothes at the mosque and started fighting police officers when they came to arrest her. Incidents like these earned Sherri a reputation as "crazy," and mosque members nicknamed her "Crazy Sherri" to distinguish her from other women in the community with the same name.

After Sherri became sick one year, a couple took her into their small South Central apartment about five miles from the mosque. They clothed and fed her until the husband went to prison for a parole violation and the wife, overwhelmed by her own mental health problems, couldn't provide care. Sherri left the couple's apartment, but where she went next no one knew.

A few months later, the imam announced that Sherri had passed. He didn't share the cause of her death, choosing instead to focus on the community's responsibility to ensure that she received a proper Muslim burial. Because she was estranged from her family, including her siblings and grown children, there was no one willing to take care of the disposition. Sherri's remains were held at the county morgue for more than one month while believers scrambled to raise money. The prohibitive cost of burial plots in Los Angeles meant that the mosque could only afford a space for Sherri that was far out from the city center, nearly ninety miles away. Yet even this lower price was no small fund-raising feat in light of members' constrained resources and the organization's precarious financial standing—nearly eight thousand dollars in court and funeral costs. Their intense efforts to provide this burial care made members feel like kin. I've been studying people who die and go unclaimed in Los Angeles in the time since finishing my fieldwork at MAQ. Across the hundreds of cases that I have researched, I have not found another religious community that went through as much to claim and bury a member as MAQ did for Sister Sherri. It's an amazing example of how the community deepens its piety through collective action both *because of* and *in spite of* its poverty.

*   *   *

One week after Ava's janaza, I was back at home in Houston and, for the first time since her death, deep enough in sleep to dream. And a vivid one it was. I dreamt that Elijah and I were following Ava as she rushed to get plastic containers filled with homemade dinners and cakes set up to sell after jumah. She moved at a feverish pace, rushing down the streets. Then suddenly, she was racing around the mosque. The dream came in flashes, like a child's animated flip book. Elijah and I were trying to catch up to Ava, to tell her she no longer had to work so hard, no longer had to skip sleep to earn another dollar. But Ava kept going, kept hustling, just as she had in life. So I kept following, as I had while she was still here. I wanted to stop her and explain that the struggle was over, that now she could go to Paradise and finally rest. But every time I reached for Ava, my hand escaped her. I was grabbing at a ghost. I tried to scream to get her attention, but no words came out. I felt helpless. I couldn't bring her back to life, and I didn't have the heart to tell her she was dead. I woke up in a sweat, heart pounding in my chest and tears starting to fill my eyes. The dream seemed to be an omen, a reminder to capture what was at the heart of Ava's story and those of so many believers at MAQ.

Sister Ava worked hard to live a Muslim way of life in South Central.

The empty cans of energy drinks cluttering the recycle shelf in her kitchen, which her siblings blamed for the heart attack, were evidence of her drive to stay up all night baking cakes. On the night she died, she was striving to earn an extra forty dollars. Ava was saving that spring in the hope she'd be able to move out of her late mother's house and finally get some peace away from her siblings. Her death underscores the harsh reality of a lifetime of hard work: there is only so much any one person can do at the individual level to surpass the boundaries of unequal structures, such as poverty and racism. For systemic change, we need systemic solutions. Still, believers want to be helped in ways that allow them to continue on a path toward righteousness, because their goals extend beyond this life. Ava wasn't ready to leave this world, but her last words—Allahu Akbar—capture the moral strength she found in Islam. They were the same words spoken by the men who were shot by police during a standoff at MAQ in the 1960s, as Malcolm X recounted in his eulogy for a slain brother.

If one thing remains constant over the decades of this community, it is belief in God and the greatness of God. That belief motivates members to keep giving when they have nothing left to give; to work hard to support their families without taking what they perceive as moral shortcuts; and to stay rooted in South Central when everything there looks and feels uprooted. Belief keeps members together, loving and laughing after tears and disagreements. Like the lead character in *Life of Pi* says, "You cannot know the strength of your faith until it's been tested." As for Sister Ava, whom I never had the chance to say goodbye to, I have no doubt that she is working hard right this moment, hustling so heaven can be even better for everyone in it. And making the angels laugh with her dirty jokes along the way.

Methods Appendix

Let's face it. We're undone by each other. And if we're not,
we're missing something.

JUDITH BUTLER, "Violence, Mourning, Politics" (2003)

Gaining access to a mosque for sociological research requires ethical sensitivity and patience, particularly for non-Muslim researchers, but it's easier than people may think. Just as anyone may attend an iftar at Masjid al-Quran, so, too, everyone is welcome to attend jumah. It was gaining access to believers that proved more difficult. Since 9/11, news stories have emerged about the placement of undercover US law enforcement officers in mosques across the country, including accounts of FBI informants at a Southern California Islamic center that had leaked to the press around the same time I started my fieldwork.[1]

Before I set foot on the grounds of MAQ, I called its leaders to explain my research interests and secure their consent. I spoke with a man I would later come to know as Fareed Jr.—son of the masjid treasurer and manager. I explained my intentions, and Fareed Jr. said I was welcome to stop by anytime, though he warned me that some in the community would not like my being there. "Don't mind them," he advised, because anyone has the right to attend the masjid, and I had the leaders' expressed permission as well. I was nervous about how I would be perceived, taking extra care to dress conservatively and always wear my black head scarf (I would later be teased for wearing lots of black and looking so serious). I believe that the staff appreciated my wearing respectful clothing without having to be asked; for that routine, it helped that I had experience in other mosques.

One month before I started gathering data at Masjid al-Quran, I had begun observing a larger, Arab-led Islamic center in another part of the

city. The center was populated by first- and second-generation Muslim immigrants from the Middle East, South Asia, and Africa, so the organization had created civic programs designed to help recent immigrants learn
their rights and obligations within the US legal system. I intended to com-
pare my findings at this center with data gathered at MAQ, which I started
alternating visits to, in order to understand how racial and class differences
shape both the lived experience of Islam and the construction of a diverse
American ummah. However, four months into the research I realized I
would never gain unplanned access to the men's areas in the Islamic center, limiting my ability to capture unscripted happenings among brothers.
By contrast, at MAQ my first visit took place inside the men's prayer area in
an informal focus group with Fareed Jr. and Sister Mira, Naeem's ex-wife.
On my second visit, I spent an entire day playing dominoes and talking
with a handful of brothers, learning pieces of their life histories. As I never
planned for the study to be only of Muslim women, just before the start of
Ramadan in August 2008 I shifted my focus to zoom in on MAQ and the
interactions I observed there.

One of the unique—and inspiring—characteristics of gender relations
at this particular site was how openly men and women interacted in public. During these interactions, certain "group styles" came into play that
reveal shared assumptions about Islamically appropriate modes of gender
behavior.[2] Women talked openly with men on the concrete sidewalks surrounding the prayer hall, inside the masjid kitchen and offices, and in the
parking lot.[3] Women and men participated together in the marketplace
after jumah, shopping at the same booths and eating together at the picnic tables. Men and women frequently hugged and even kissed the other's
cheek as friendly gestures, especially if they hadn't seen each other for an
extended time. These interaction patterns suggested that I would be able to
offer a fuller portrait of community life than many ethnographic studies of
orthodox religious communities, which tend to focus on the participants
whose gender aligns with the researcher's.[4]

Once I narrowed my field site to MAQ, I committed to participate in its
community life as much as possible. For the first five years of fieldwork, I
attended weekly religious services, volunteered on planning committees,
cooked with sisters in the masjid kitchen, and hung out with believers at the
masjid day and night. I spent the first several months of the study focused
on building rapport with believers by simply being present and answering
their repeated questions about my intentions. During this period, each time
I left the site I immediately jotted field notes or dictated my observations
into an audio recorder I kept in my car. Then I transcribed and expanded
these observations into complete field notes upon returning to my office or

home. As believers grew more accustomed to my presence and started referring to me as Sister Pam, I began to take observational notes in public view. I use quotes for dialogue I recorded as it happened or just after.

During my first Ramadan at MAQ, I spent thirty of its thirty-one nights at the masjid, participating in the nightly iftar dinner and staying through Taraweeh prayers after dark and often well into the night. I further demonstrated the seriousness of my commitment to the community by sponsoring iftar that first year with Brother Naeem. In subsequent years, I sponsored on my own or cosponsored with other sisters. In total, I attended more than 120 iftar dinners across the ten years of my field work. In many ways, iftar provided the perfect setting to interview people without the awkwardness of a formal interview format. Over plates of halal soul food, I exchanged stories with believers about our experiences growing up, religious beliefs, political perspectives, and more mundane activities like retail and food preferences. From these conversations, I learned about the community's sense of shared history, common understandings about how the organization operated, and perceptions of its neighborhood both then and over time. I collected life histories of many regular attendees and often reflected on this data to understand the historical significance of believers' experiences in the Nation of Islam.

In August 2009, I decided to move to the neighborhood to better immerse myself in both the MAQ community and everyday life in South Central. I struggled to find an apartment I could rent, because many of the listings were in Spanish. Though I spoke some Spanish, I didn't feel confident negotiating a lease in the language. This was during my second Ramadan at the masjid, and I hoped I could call on some of the members for help. By that time, I had been receiving more invitations to events and gatherings outside the mosque, suggesting to me that I was gaining more acceptance in the community. But when I tried to draw from my connections at the masjid to find a place to live, knowing that some of the believers were landlords, I came up empty-handed. Brother Naeem recommended an agent he knew, but after I spoke with her I realized she didn't specialize in the area around the masjid. When I told Naeem this, he asked, "You want to go deep into the 'hood?" I said yes, and that my first preference was to rent a room from a believer. He shook his head and said, "People respect you, but you push it too far." I asked him why it was pushing if I needed a room and someone wanted the cash. Then he tried, in a somewhat roundabout way, to say that I was a target and that I made other people a target.

I pressed further. "Why?"

Naeem reached out and touched my bare wrist, gliding his finger back and forth three times by way of emphasizing the color of my skin. "Because of that." He said he had a room, but, "God, if something happened to you . . ." Then he shook his head. "People will feel bad if you get hurt." Naeem didn't live in the immediate neighborhood, something I learned later. At that point, it was enough that he was a divorced man and I an unmarried woman. I knew that our living together would have been inappropriate in a community that deeply values marriage and sexual propriety.

Eventually, I located a room advertised on Craigslist and moved in with a Mexican American family. Believers found this odd. They said I should have gone through the Muslims. I remember feeling that I was an accepted nuisance but still had miles to go before I would feel like a member of the community.

During my time as a neighborhood resident, I volunteered as a tutor at a youth center, helping students from local elementary schools with their homework. I've never lived anywhere else that had as much pride of place and sense of community. The networks of believers in the neighborhood who offered me support were an amazing source of strength, making up for the more aggravating aspects of life in a depressed urban zone. I could have stayed longer, but in September 2010 I had to move out of the room I was renting because the living situation had become unsafe (reasons unrelated to MAQ). I found a house to rent in a different part of South LA, closer to where some of the wealthier MAQ members lived. The neighborhood was majority Black or African American (68 percent) with a poverty rate less than half that of the area around the masjid, but at just over 20 percent a rate still high compared with other parts of the city. Living in this second neighborhood, not far from the famous Crenshaw district, allowed me to observe how believers with middle-class status utilized the mosque in ways different from those who lived in MAQ's neighborhood. I stayed in this home, building a family there with my partner and later our daughter, until leaving LA in June 2015.

From August 2013 until May 2015, I made regular visits to MAQ but without the same level of intensity as in my first five years. By this time, my relationships with several members had involved spending time together outside the mosque more than in it. Also, after the dramas of 2012 that I recounted in chapter 3, I found my time at MAQ becoming more emotionally exhausting. I decided to cut down on the amount of fieldwork to focus on writing. However, I could not let go of the community completely; it had become too much a part of me and my life in LA. I found myself getting drawn back into its collective effervescence. When I left LA in June 2015 following my graduation—which Sisters Ava and Aisha, along with Aisha's youngest daughter, attended—I continued to make quarterly visits for another three years (including at least once per Ramadan). The continued contact was possible because of fieldwork for another project that brought me regularly to LA.

Ethnographers are usually quite adept at outlining their fieldwork and note-taking procedures in detail—at explaining how they analyzed, less so. So let me take a moment to explain how I proceeded from the thousands of jottings I made in the field to produce a book. First, I use an abductive approach to data analysis and theory construction.[5] Abductive analysis involves an iterative process of working with data in connection with diverse literatures.[6] I was interested in understanding the everyday experiences of MAQ members, with particular attention to how living in a disadvantaged urban context interacted with believers' constructions of Islam. As I read my data in light of the existing literature on American Islam, I was repeatedly struck by how different the problems believers expressed were from those reported by respondents in studies of South Asian and Arab American Muslims. For example, when I asked believers at MAQ to explain how their lives had changed since 9/11, they recognized that discrimination was greater against immigrant Muslims but insisted that little had changed for African American Muslims, with the exception that they found it more difficult to receive money wired from overseas Muslim organizations. The more common response, captured best in the words of one sister: "We were Black before 9/11, and Black after." Comments like this, which came early in my fieldwork, pointed me to read more broadly to understand the racial, class, and spatial inequalities that would frame such a response. Yet while 9/11 was not a significant turning point for believers at MAQ, their transition from the Nation of Islam to Sunni Islam proved pivotal, standing as an important point of departure from other Muslim Americans. I consistently found that what had taken place at MAQ thirty years earlier continued to shape how believers interpreted Islam, organized contemporary community life, and understood themselves in relation to other Muslims.

Throughout the book, I draw heavily from hundreds of informal in situ interviews but few formal ones. This was done for two reasons. First, due to the heightened surveillance of Muslims in the United States since 9/11, before starting fieldwork I made a choice, in consultation with the Institutional Review Board at the University of California, Los Angeles, not to use an audio recorder while inside the mosque. It worked well that I could buy cassette tapes or CDs of khutbahs. Second, for the few times I interviewed believers formally in their homes or at restaurants, I found that their speech styles and content changed considerably when I turned on the recorder (always with their consent). This made me skeptical about the added value of formal interviews for research aiming at long-term immersion and everyday happenings. Instead, the informal interview technique became my go-to form of asking follow-up questions or clarifying certain points when I wanted to better understand the motivations of individual members. Per the IRB, I changed members' names to protect their privacy.

Intersecting Positionalities

To anyone who has taken a sociology or an anthropology class, it may seem unrealistic to believe what a white woman writes about an African American community, especially one that had once been part of a Black nationalist movement. I am well aware of the tensions my race creates, and I wrestled with how to address these tensions throughout my fieldwork. In this way, I think it helped that I was studying a race-conscious community that felt comfortable calling me out on my privilege, as Naeem did the day of a barbeque fund-raiser I attended on my second visit to MAQ. "What's it like to grow up privileged?" he asked me while we sat on the steps of the masjid. I fumbled my way through an answer, telling him that I didn't grow up with money and that I had to earn my way to college with a merit scholarship. I was too nervous to look at Naeem for a reaction. When his phone rang, I said a silent prayer of thanks and quickly changed the subject once he was off the call.

The next many years were an on-the-ground education about what it means to grow up privileged. Now I understand better how my status as a white, Christian-raised, college-degreed woman offers me a path through life that, while it doesn't always feel easy, is undeniably and significantly easier than the paths of the women and men at Masjid al-Quran. Even believers of relative wealth were subject to greater threats due to America's trenchant racial inequities in policing and surveillance. By contrast, I could travel through the neighborhood without feeling at danger from police or local gangs, and I could shed the stress of living in a poor neighborhood when I drove off in my modest but reliable ten-year-old Honda sedan to attend class or teach at UCLA. In those hours away from the neighborhood, I could lose myself in a world unencumbered by the threats characterizing everyday life in South Central.

It's not easy to know how to talk about race or class in everyday life, but I believe that people in privileged categories are obligated to try to better understand what status affords them as well as what that status closes off to nondominant groups, to pull from Weber's classic language. The onus is on the privileged to learn—not on the already overburdened communities to explain how, why, or when difference matters and with what consequences. At moments in this book, I share my thoughts and feelings where I think an opportunity exists to break down assumptions and stereotypes. I retell the honest, albeit difficult, conversations about race, class, and religion that

I had with believers at MAQ, including occasions when I fumbled, in the hopes that these conversations will generate discussions among readers, especially students. I am grateful that Naeem, a fellow educator, called me out on my privilege, as uncomfortable as it was in the moment, because it made me see this hard truth early in my fieldwork.

At the same time, race was not always the most salient category of difference between the believers at MAQ and me. Often, it was faith that had more observable impacts on my positioning within the community. Indeed, in ethnographies of religious communities it's important to see positionality as intersectional and identities as multiple.[7] I entered the field with humility about my knowledge of Islam, demonstrating this humility through deference and respect. Like Su'ad Abdul Khabeer, I chose to see believers as my "teachers"—they were the experts and I their student.[8] My enthusiasm for learning about the community may have confused some people into thinking I was asking questions because I might convert. To avoid misleading people, in the first several years I opted not to pray. Brother Fareed asked me about this one day, and when I explained my position, he laughed. "Salat doesn't make you a *Mooslem*." In later years, I followed the sisters as they made salat, though not as often as they would have liked. By then, I had been accustomed to catching up on field notes during prayer time.

As time went on and my involvement in the community grew deeper and more complicated, I considered conversion. I wanted desperately to be a part of *this* community—not to get more immersed in a scholarly sense but because I loved the idea of being attached to a community with such history and depth of ties. Like the famous song from the 1980s sitcom *Cheers*, it was seductive to be at a place where everybody knows your name, especially in a city that can be alienating for newcomers and longtime residents alike. Some believers felt strongly that I should want to convert, occasionally cornering me in the kitchen to ask, "When you gonna take your *shahada*, sister?" The *shahada* is the declaration of faith within Islam; it requires only two lines, recited in Arabic: "La ilaha illa'llah. Muhammadun rasul Allah" (There is no God but God. Muhammad is the messenger of God). I believe what the first line says, but going beyond it to recite the second line wasn't something I could do with ethical consciousness. For that, I think my roots in Christianity remained too strong for me. I am not religious in general, and I feel uncomfortable talking about my faith. I would rather be left alone to believe in God and pray when I feel like it. But in the interest of full methodological disclosure and general fairness since I was studying a religious community, I felt it was important to be honest with believers when they asked about my beliefs and personal religious history. I believe it's the right thing to do the same now with readers.

Race and religion were two categories I knew I'd need to be reflexive about as I entered the project—but motherhood was not. However, three years into my fieldwork I became pregnant and, once visibly so, was thrown into a new set of relations to navigate. For the most part, members were ecstatic, asking how I felt and, after my daughter was born, asking how she was doing and why I didn't bring her along more. Among the sisters, I had a sense that I had finally earned status as an adult (despite being in my late twenties when I started fieldwork). A handful of members openly criticized me for being an unwed mother, finding it haram (like Sheikh Burhan did in chapter 4). For this small subpopulation, I had to renegotiate what was ethical for my observations. Sister Lisa, for example, distanced herself from me, and we stopped hanging out when others weren't around. She refused to tell me exactly why, but I heard rumors from other sisters that Lisa thought it was inappropriate that I chose to have a child without marrying the father. I decided not to impose myself into situations where my presence might make her uncomfortable, and from that point forward I observed her family from a distance. Overall, I think motherhood made me a better ethnographer and sociologist, helping me develop greater sensitivity to the struggles of the believers, especially sisters raising families on their own.

Between my race, religion, and changing constructions of womanhood, I learned to see data collection and analysis more clearly as intersectional processes that require ongoing critical reflection to understand how one's personal background affects the interpretation of data. This includes the gendered, racial, and religious lenses through which we see and experience the world but also how we theoretically make sense of it. Ethnographers Stefan Timmermans and Iddo Tavory write, "The disposition to perceive the world and its surprises—including the very reflection on one's positions in this world—is predicated on the researcher's biography as well as on an affinity and familiarity with broader theoretical fields."[9] In other words, what we read and whom we take classes with in graduate school directly impact our analysis and what kind of scholar we are. They advise scholars to see data analysis in qualitative research as involving a kind of theoretical positionality. After this project, I know that social science is for me a necessarily ethnographic endeavor. I can't imagine doing research that does not involve getting "on the ground" to see for myself what people are doing and saying. Like the abductive analytical approach that I used in data analysis, which involves an iterative process of moving between data and theory in search of surprising findings, I went back and forth between my multiple, overlapping positions in the field and those in the classroom.[10] This process was a sort of "dual abductive analysis"—applying the logic of abduction to find the unexpected ways I was changing and being changed by the fieldwork.

Writing Ethnography after a Loss

It's been nearly three years since the passing of Sister Ava, and I still tear up when I write about her. I find it harder in many ways to be at home writing than back at her house, at the mosque, or traveling the streets of the neighborhood, all spaces where we spent time together. When I'm in South Central, I can feel her presence; but alone at my computer, I have nothing except field notes, memories, and sadness. For me, the most difficult part of the ethnographic project has always been how to capture the emotions of others I observed. In the translation of field observations into sociological analysis, it often feels as though I've lost something. Now the challenges of writing are compounded by grief over a loved one unexpectedly gone from my life, the shock of Ava's death relived each time I write about her. It helps that I must use a pseudonym, but that emotional padding is stripped away within seconds when I put myself back in time through my ethnographic memory making. As I did throughout the project, I aimed to use my personal experiences not as data but as heuristics devices to ask questions of my data. I developed a kind of emotional positionality that helped me be more sensitive to believers as complicated human beings.[11]

In sociology, we tend to measure a person's worth in material terms or try to describe his or her place in society based on concepts we think will enable easier comparison (capital, networks, status, attainment, mobility, etc.). As a result, we often fail to capture the unquantifiable ways that people impact one another. Take Brother Fareed, for example. A conventional sociological analysis might look at his long-term unemployment, his lack of formal education, his divorces, his strained relations with his sons, his estrangement from his daughters, and his criminal record as signs of a life defined by disadvantage and social isolation. Without ethnography, we wouldn't know his lived impact on others, including the dedication he gave to the mosque community, how "this was his life" (per Dina's words), or the fact that his death was mourned by hundreds of people. These are not weak, strong, or disposable ties but ties of human connection. Ties reminding us that life is made more meaningful when we spend it doing things together. To paraphrase Judith Butler, if we're not undone by each other, then something is missing. Fareed and I had a complicated relationship. At times he would openly criticize me, but other times he stood up for me. It was similar with Ava. She was the first to tell me when I was getting a little "thick" (putting on weight) or being judgmental, but also one of the first visitors—along with Sister Aisha—who came to the hospital after I gave birth to my daughter. As affected as I was by their deaths, the crinkled pages in my field notebook a reminder of the tears I shed for both, I know that the believers at MAQ, who had known Fareed and Ava decades longer, experienced a depth of emotional loss that undid them. Sister Aisha, for one, has yet to process the loss of her best friend nearly three years later. Ethnography is the best (perhaps the only) method for doing justice to the complicated relationships of a community like MAQ's, where believers' lives are entwined with emotion and history. I am eternally grateful for their willingness to entwine me with them, and I pray that I have done justice to the complicated beauty of their ties.

Acknowledgments

This book would not exist without the Masjid al-Quran community. I extend my thanks and gratitude to the women and men of that community who put up with my questions and note taking for more years than any of us planned and who today offer hugs when I visit. It pains me that I can't use your real names, but I have no doubt that as you read these pages you'll know exactly who you are and, I hope, recognize the enduring admiration I have for your community. Special thanks to Sisters Ava and Aisha for their love, support, and motherly protection over the years. I will forever miss our late-night movie marathons inside the masjid and our adventures around town in Ava's van, but I take comfort in knowing that these moments will always be with me. Ava changed me at my core. I think about her every day. Thank you also to my dear friend Shaheedah, who has grown into an amazing young woman in the decade I have known her. Although she was too young at the start of this project to be included as a main "character," she provides me with much-needed "real-life" motivation. My hope is that she (and thousands of young women and men like her) will experience a life filled with greater opportunities than previous generations of South Central's young people have had.

I am indebted to Stefan Timmermans for his support over the years. Stefan read multiple chapter drafts, his comments ripe with thoughtful critique and care. Though the words on these pages are my own, his voice appears in the way I think as a sociologist and ethnographer ("if you don't write it in your fieldnotes, it never happened!"). Like the other Timmermaniacs, I have aspired to live up to the high standards he sets for both himself and his students. Thank you also for making sure I get my nautical metaphors right and for becoming an inspiring collaborator on the Unclaimed project. I've also benefited from the mentorship of Elaine Howard Ecklund, who has helped guide my career. She and the entire team in the Religion and Public Life Program at Rice University, including Laura Achenbaum and Hayley Hemstreet, provided a welcoming home for me to rethink this book and to reexamine what kind of scholar I want to be. A special shout-out to Jim Elliott for the thought-provoking walks around campus. I'm a better urban scholar because of you. Thank you also to Jenifer Bratter and Sergio Chavez for the friendly lunches and talks at Rice.

Karen Leonard was an advocate for this project from the beginning, and I am deeply grateful for her support on earlier drafts. Mignon Moore offered the right mixes of humor and honesty at key moments in the long process of graduate study. And Bill Roy was instrumental in helping me shape my sociological imagination through his teaching and mentoring.

At the University of Chicago Press, I wish to thank my amazing editor, Kyle Wagner, and his editorial associate, Dylan Montanari. Kyle understood what I wanted to do with this book, sometimes better than I did. Thank you for believing in me. To the rest of the team at the Press—Ruth Goring, Sandra Hazel, and Adrienne Meyers—a warm thank-you for making the editorial and promotion processes smooth. I also owe a tremendous debt of gratitude to the two readers, Melissa Wilde and an anonymous reader, who reviewed the manuscript. I was overwhelmed by their expressions of clear joy in studying it.

Though Alison MacKeen did not represent me for this book, the feedback she offered on another project has undoubtedly strengthened my writing. Thanks, Alison. I'm also honored to have worked with Caroline Lester and Seki Shiwoku, who provided helpful comments after reading the manuscript in its entirety.

I have benefited from the support and advice of many friends and colleagues over the decade it took to research and write this book. A special thank-you to Marie Berry, Sarah Bracke, Marci Cottingham, Gordon Douglas, Nahoko Kameo, Sarah Lakhani, Iddo Tavory, Linda van de Kamp, and Adeola Enigbokan. Adeola was the best colleague and friend I could have had at the University of Amsterdam, where I finished writing the manuscript. It hasn't been easy living so far from the communities that inspire and nurture me, and I leaned heavily on Adeola's social science wit and New Yorker sarcasm. Thank you for reminding me to go wholeheartedly into everything I do.

Last but not least, I would like to thank my family and closest friends, especially the sisterhood that has lifted me up for decades. For more than twenty-five years, Dona Kim Murphey and Prisidha Avril de Guzman have encouraged me to pursue my dreams without doubt or judgment. I am truly grateful for their love and friendship. I believe in both of them and would give my life to prove it. Thank you also to Suzie Dewey, who opened my eyes to a life outside the United States and the joys of indulging my wanderlust; Katerina Papadapoulous, whose laughter always brightens my day; Tiffany Thompson, who shares a love for South Central; and, importantly, Andrea Ott, who provides a lifeline to America with her weekly calls and her offers of an air mattress in LA whenever I need it. Andrea folded obituary programs with me on the eve of one of the hardest days of my life. I am blessed to have a friend with a heart as true as hers.

Thank you to my parents, my grandmother, and my in-laws. A special note of appreciation to my partner, Ejaz, who patiently accepted that "one more hour" in the field often turned into three or four and who agreed to raise our family closer to the mosque.

During this project I became a mother, a personal transformation that also changed me professionally. I believe I'm a better sociologist as a result of having taken on the awesome responsibility of molding another person's social and moral foundation. Thank you, Sariya, for making me laugh every day. I am forever by your side.

Notes

Introduction

The dedication page contains a verse from a sura, or chapter from the Qur'an, that I copied from a prayer schedule flyer produced by Masjid al-Quran. In general, I quote or reference only suras and hadiths (traditions of Muhammad and his companions) that were used by members of the community.

1. Accessed March 30, 2020, at https://www.psychologytoday.com/us/blog/the-tao-inno vation/201211/meaning-faith-and-the-life-pi.

2. Wadud 2006, 92; emphasis added.

3. Wadud 2006, 93.

4. Mahmood 2005.

5. Bautista 2008, 79.

6. Mahmood 2005, 158.

7. Mahmood 2005, 158.

8. Mahmood 2001.

9. Wadud 2006, 39.

10. Leonard 2003; Wilde and Tevington 2017.

11. Sociologist Melissa Wilde (2017) terms this intersection of religion and overlapping systems of inequality "complex religion."

12. Emerson 2006.

13. Costa Vargas 2006.

14. I borrow the term *chosen family* from queer and feminist studies. A chosen family is a family unit "defined by intentionality, identity, and community connection rather than biological relation" (Hammack, Frost, and Hughes 2019, 580).

15. Prickett 2018.

16. Pew Research Center 2018.

17. Notable exceptions include Mary Patillo's *Black Picket Fences* (1999) and *Black on the Block* (2007).

18. Gregory 1998; Hunter et al. 2016.

19. Hunter et al. 2016, 32.

20. Hunter et al. 2016, 34.

21. Tavory 2016.

22. Avishai 2008.

23. See Orsi's (2003) work on lived religion in the city for a detailed discussion.

24. Wolfe 2003.

25. Wolfe 2003.

26. I follow the lead of Su'ad Abdul Khabeer (2016), who uses *teachers* to refer to her research participants and interlocutors.

27. Ammerman 2014.

28. Ammerman 2014.

29. Pew Research Center 2010.

30. Pew Research Center 2017.

31. Pew Research Center 2017.

32. Prickett 2018.

33. Bagby, Pearl, and Froehle 2001.

34. Anderson 1999.

35. While many at MAQ came through the Nation of Islam, they have never seen themselves as part of that group, which was featured in "The Hate That Hate Produced," a 1959 CBS documentary that brought the Nation to national attention. At the same time, community members hold tight to the particularism of the African American Muslim experience as one that should be protected. This particularism is well documented by earlier ethnographers of African American Islam, including Carolyn Rouse, Jamillah Karim, Zain Abdullah, and Su'ad Abdul Khabeer.

Chapter One

1. Siddiqi 2014.

2. Winchester 2008.

3. Winchester 2008, 1769.

4. See Borden 2012 and Nazish 2014.

5. Believers used two terms to refer to charitable giving: *zakat* and *sadaqa*. Zakat is one of the five core pillars of Islam and is commonly understood as a "tax" on personal wealth (customarily 2.5% of one's total capital). Though it can be paid annually, I saw believers spread out their obligation by making small payments throughout the year, encouraged by religious leaders to do so if a one-time flat payment wasn't possible. *Sadaqa* at MAQ typically referred to additional forms of charity beyond zakat. Some scholars of Islam argue that zakat is intended to help needy Muslims only, reserving *sadaqa* for helping non-Muslims (Laird and Cadge 2009).

6. I participated actively in six Ramadans at MAQ, from 2008 to 2013. I have since visited at least one iftar per year. During my fieldwork, Ramadan fell during the summer months, when daylight hours are longer.

7. Smith 2010.

8. In the earlier years of my project, the imams used the same procedure to determine when to hold the Eid al-Fitr celebration to conclude the fast, though toward the end of my fieldwork it seemed that the imams were starting to split into their own factions.

9. Mahmood 2005, 49.

10. Zerubavel 1989, 2003.

11. Winchester 2008, 1769.

12. Tavory 2016, 2018.

13. Beoku-Betts 1995.

14. GhaneaBassiri 2013.

15. Putnam 2001, 23.

16. McRoberts 2003.

17. McRoberts 2003, 83.
18. McRoberts 2003.
19. McRoberts 2003, 67.
20. McRoberts 2003; Tavory 2016.
21. I attended another masjid for four months before focusing on MAQ. During that time, I signed up for the organization's listserv, which I received throughout the study. The figure of $1,400 comes from emails sent to potential sponsors on the list.
22. Singer 2008, 78.
23. Singer 2008, 79.
24. Stiles 2003.
25. Stiles 2003.
26. Mahmood 2005, 34.
27. Mahmood 2005, 34.
28. Sullivan 2012, 15.
29. Venkatesh 1997.
30. Venkatesh 1997, 90.
31. Stuart 2016.
32. I independently suspected this about the bodega soon after starting my fieldwork, so I asked Sister Ava what she knew about the store. I didn't share my suspicions, just noted with curiosity how busy the bodega always seemed to be. She smiled, seemingly proud of my observation, and remarked, "You noticed." Then she told me that anytime you see "that many Mexicans and blacks together, they're up to something." I knew that Ava had sons who previously sold drugs in the neighborhood and that she was well versed on which gangs controlled different areas, so I trusted her take on the bodega. Yet Ava didn't worry, nor did other believers who talked about the corner as a pocket of crime (St. Jean 2007). In these conversations, no one at MAQ expressed concern about the men or the bodega, nor did they think suspected criminal activities would spread. I asked Brother Fareed from the main office why, and he simply said, "They know better." He then shared that the mosque once caught a bodega employee smoking weed in the alley behind the mosque and alerted Red, the group's leader. According to Fareed, guys from the store beat up the worker, and the mosque had had no problems since.
33. Tavory 2010, 53.
34. McRoberts 2003.
35. Anderson 1999.
36. Sherman 2009.
37. Sherman 2009, 180.
38. Stack 1974.
39. Lamont 2000.
40. Hunter 2013, 208.

Chapter Two

1. Imam Mohammed was born Wallace D. Muhammad and changed his name to Warith Deen Mohammed after dismantling the Nation of Islam that he inherited from his late father.
2. A *dua* is an act of supplication. MAQ used the term to refer to a prayer that asks Allah for something: blessings, improved health, etc.
3. Williams 2011; Wolfe 2003.
4. The term *pioneer* refers to members who came through "the First," or the Nation of Islam.
5. DeCaro 1996, 21.

6. Essien-Udom 1962.

7. According to Lincoln (1994 [1961]), opponents of Elijah Muhammad pushed Fard out of the Detroit temple and to Chicago, while Essien-Udom (1962) describes Fard and his disciple as going together. Both scholars portray the movement as one in flux until Muhammad took definitive control and raised the Nation's economic profile, with the latter becoming emblematic of Muhammad's strategy for organizational growth.

8. DeCaro 1996, 28.

9. Lincoln 1994 [1961], 68–69.

10. Lincoln 1994 [1961], 68–69.

11. Essien-Udom 1962.

12. Gibson and Karim 2014, 10.

13. Kelley 1994.

14. Lincoln 1994 [1961], 120.

15. Scott 1985.

16. Curtis 2002, 72.

17. Sides 2003; Turner 1997.

18. Sides 2003, 113.

19. Sides 2003, 113.

20. Lincoln 1994 [1961], 24.

21. Dawson 2001, 108.

22. Sides 2003, 174.

23. Sides 2003, 173.

24. Sides 2003, 173.

25. Sides 2003.

26. I transcribed the words from a clip of Malcolm X speaking at the funeral, included in a DVD documentary made about the community by one of its members.

27. Turner 1997, 206.

28. This came from an interview in the same documentary cited above.

29. The Watts riots led to thirty-four deaths, over one thousand reported injuries, and property damage estimated at $40 million (J. Abu-Lughod 2007, 213).

30. Lincoln 1994 [1961], 264.

31. Lincoln 1994 [1961], 264; also Gardell 1996.

32. Lincoln 1994 [1961], 89.

33. Lincoln 1994 [1961], 263.

34. Curtis 2002, 113.

35. Curtis 2002, 113.

36. Precise figures for the Nation's membership are impossible to know. The organization was, as part of its written creed, secretive and would often exaggerate its numbers. Figures ranged from a few thousand to thirty thousand. Regardless, the organization was large enough and Muhammad powerful enough that the FBI targeted the NOI in its COINTELPRO operations. See Curtis 2002, 112; also Gardell 1996.

37. Imam Mohammed also wanted believers to fulfill their religious obligation of making the holy pilgrimage called *hajj* so they could strengthen their authority on Islam. In 1976, he took three hundred people to Mecca and selected Khalid to lead one of the delegations—a trip sponsored by the royal family of Saudi Arabia. *Hajj* became a new marker of religious commitment, but even with their relative financial improvement, few of MAQ's members could afford the costly trips. Working-class and poorer members came to rely on immigrant Muslim sponsors to finance their pilgrimages, highlighting critical class disparities between the two Muslim populations.

38. Gardell 1996, 117.

39. Mamiya 1982, 146.

40. Kun and Pulido 2013.

41. Kun and Pulido 2013.

42. The growth of the county's Latino population then continued, such that now Latinos comprise nearly half (48.3 percent) of *all* county residents, while the percentage of African Americans is in single digits 9.4 percent. Perhaps more telling, the number of African Americans residing within the city limits has grown by just over sixteen thousand in nearly forty years (Kun and Pulido 2013).

43. Wilson 1987, 1996; but see also Small 2008.

44. Sides 2012, 44; Wacquant 2008.

45. Sides 2003, 114.

46. J. Abu-Lughod 2007; Grant, Oliver, and James 1996; Laslett 1996; Sides 2003.

47. Costa Vargas 2006; Davis 1990.

48. Costa Vargas 2006, 58.

49. Flory, Loskota, and Miller 2011.

50. Prickett 2014, 223.

51. Prickett 2014, 224.

52. The neighborhood was never 100 percent Black, but believers often recalled a past in which South Central was "all Black"; see Prickett 2014.

Chapter Three

1. Women use the scarves to cover their heads, but I do not use the term *hijab* here, because the scarves were not specifically Muslim (i.e., not veils per se). They were the types of fashionable scarves in different prints and colors that one could find in a retail shop.

2. Zelizer 2010.

3. Roussell 2015.

4. I transcribed his exact words using an audio recording of the khutbah, which I purchased from the masjid for five dollars.

5. Nelson 2005.

6. Cf. Venkatesh 2006.

7. Thieme 2018, 541; emphasis added.

8. Thieme 2018, 541.

9. Thieme 2018, 541.

10. P. Ong et al. 2017.

11. Gibson and Karim 2014, 63.

12. Curtis 2006, 12.

13. Gibson and Karim 2014, 64.

14. For more on Islamic liberation theology, see Kahera 2002.

15. Khabeer 2016, 61.

16. Mol, Moser, and Pols 2010, 14.

17. Nembhard 2014.

18. Erikson 1978.

19. Erikson 1978, 82.

20. The Jungle is what locals call the area of Baldwin Village in South Central, a set of low-income apartment complexes notorious for gang and drug activity and related violence (Hunt 2010, 6).

21. Goffman 1952.

22. Stack (1974) found a similar strategy of ambiguity.
23. Wolfe 2003.
24. Stack 1974, 39.
25. Stack 1974, 39.
26. Stack 1974, 43.
27. Harris-Lacewell 2004.
28. Chaddha and Wilson 2011, 165.
29. Hochschild 2016, 135.
30. Mol, Moser, and Pols 2010.

Chapter Four

1. Haddad, Smith, and Moore 2006; Inglehart and Norris 2003; Korteweg 2008; A. Ong 1995.
2. Mahmood 2005, 189; see also L. Abu-Lughod 2002.
3. See also Rouse 2004.
4. Stack 1974.
5. Sullivan 2012.
6. While at different times over the five years of the study I observed women forming informal religious education classes, coming together to discuss the Qur'an and to learn about important women in the Prophet Muhammad's life, the groups typically waned after a few weeks or months. These also failed to gain the authority of acknowledgment in the monthly community bulletin. Sisters' lack of mobilization at MAQ for gender-segregated learning, which is in stark contrast with the women in Mahmood's (2005) study, should not be interpreted as meaning the women were less committed to learning Islam or the Qur'an. Rather, the women were often juggling multiple work and family commitments, their everyday burdens limiting their ability to participate. By contrast, women in the Egyptian mosque movement came from the middle and elite classes, affording them the privilege of time to attend intensive Qur'anic reading groups at the mosque (Mahmood 2005).
7. Majeed 2006, 749.
8. Quoted in Gibson and Karim 2014, 7.
9. Gibson and Karim 2014.
10. Gibson and Karim 2014, 8.
11. Rouse 2004.
12. Gibson and Karim 2014, 11.
13. Gibson and Karim 2014, 12.
14. The most visible signifier of Mohammed's love for his mother was to rename the NOI school system the Clara Muhammad Elementary and Secondary School. Education became the central tenet of Imam Mohammed's blueprint for African American progress, and one that MAQ would turn to in the 1990s when faced with a critical choice whether to use its limited funds to build a new masjid or a new school. It chose the school based on Imam Mohammed's advice.
15. Quoted in Gibson and Karim 2014, 92; transcribed from a YouTube video, 9:16, published May 19, 2000, https://www.youtube.com/watch?v=Jmabcp8GUjY.
16. Anderson 1999.
17. Quoted in Gibson and Karim 2014, 99.
18. Gibson and Karim 2014, 93.
19. Abdul Aleem Seifullah, "Women: Equals? Inferiors? Superiors?" *Bilalian News*, August 25, 1977, 5. Quoted in Gibson and Karim 2014, 94.

20. Seifullah, p. 5, quoted in Gibson and Karim 2014, 94.

21. Seifullah, p. 5, quoted in Gibson and Karim 2014, 94.

22. Quoted in Gibson and Karim 2014, 94; emphasis added.

23. Gibson and Karim 2014, 91.

24. Womanist theology exists alongside a larger tradition of Black feminism, including the work of the Combahee River Collective and Black scholars like Patricia Hill Collins, although it differs by putting explicit emphasis on women's abilities to derive strength from religion and religious texts (Chan-Malik 2018, 29).

25. Chan-Malik 2018, 26.

26. Chan-Malik 2018, 26.

27. Chan-Malik 2018, 26.

28. Chan-Malik 2018, 26.

29. Emphasis added.

30. Rouse (2004) uses the phrase "separate but equal" to refer to ideas like those that Chan-Malik (2018) refers to as complementarity.

31. Dow 2015, 38. Separate spheres and the cult of domesticity emerged in the eighteenth and nineteenth centuries as measures of gendered worth for middle-class white families. Slavery and institutionalized slavery prevented Black women from being included in the ideals, as their "value" was seen by the dominant white society as related to work alongside men in the fields. "Thus, in comparison with white mothers, African American mothers occupied a different position within the American economic structure that produced different expectations about the place of work in their lives" (Dow 2015, 39). After emancipation, Black women continued to work outside the home due to economic necessity. Depending on where you fall in the feminist spectrum, African American mothers have been either "exempted" from (Dow 2015) or denied the possibility of occupying separate gendered spheres.

32. Rouse 2004, 147.

33. Gans 2011.

34. Hunter and Robinson 2016, 392.

35. Hunter and Robinson 2016.

36. Collins 2000.

37. Collins 2000, 77.

38. Collins 2000, 77.

39. Collins 2000, 69.

40. L. Abu-Lughod 2013.

41. Chan-Malik 2018, 25.

42. Chan-Malik 2018, 80.

43. Gibson and Karim 2014.

44. Rouse 2004, 51.

45. Dow 2015.

46. Rouse 2004.

47. Rehman 2007.

48. See Buddi 2018.

49. Macfarlane 2012.

50. Vatuk 2008.

51. In 2018, the Indian government passed an executive order making triple talaq a punishable offense, with men liable for up to three years in prison if convicted. The order came after the Muslim Women Protection of Rights on Marriage Bill 2017 failed in the Indian parliament.

52. One of my informants suggested that in the past, sisters had been allowed to stay at the masjid, some with their children in tow, but I never observed this. From all the information I

could gather, it has been decades since a sister lived there, although women like Ava and Aisha clearly appropriated the masjid for their own ends (Prickett 2015).

53. Stack 1974.

54. Prickett 2019.

55. Rouse 2004.

56. Hunter et al. 2016.

57. Hunter et al. 2016, 32.

58. For a critique on the use of adaptation in the literature on urban poverty, see Gregory 1998; also Venkatesh 1997. For a critique on the reduction of religion to a "coping mechanism" among poor populations, see Sullivan 2012.

59. Byng 1998.

60. Frederick 2003, 4.

61. Avishai 2016, 270.

Chapter Five

1. For more on the clothing choices of African American Muslim women, see Karim 2008.

2. Mauss 1954.

3. Baudrillard 1981, 64.

4. Kochuyt 2009, 99.

5. Smith 2010, 29.

6. Beydoun 2016, 1469.

7. Leonard 2003, 14.

8. Karim 2008, 37.

9. Bilici 2012; Love 2017.

10. Kishi 2017.

11. Love 2017, 21.

12. Love 2017, 21.

13. Love 2017, 21.

14. Bail 2014; Mohamed and O'Brien 2011.

15. Guhin 2018; O'Brien 2017.

16. Pew Research Center 2012.

17. Calhoun-Brown 1999.

18. Rouse 2004.

19. Bagby 2012.

20. Emerson 2006.

21. Karim 2008.

22. Khabeer 2016, 14.

23. Sherman Jackson outlines his perspective in detail in *Islam and the Blackamerican* (2005).

24. Khabeer 2016.

25. For more on public stereotypes of South Central, see Bennett 2010 and Hunt 1997. In her study of mosques in Chicago and Atlanta, Karim (2008) found immigrant Muslims holding similarly negative views about people in "the inner city," with South Asian immigrant women especially frank about their efforts to integrate into white rather than Black communities because of the latter's perceived lower social standing in the United States (231).

26. Malcolm X 1964, 340; emphasis added.

27. Hunt 1997.

28. Wacquant 2008.

29. Wacquant 2008, 239.
30. The concept of racial formation is from Omi and Winant 1994.
31. Karim 2008.
32. Curtis 2002; Grewal 2013.
33. Karim 2008.
34. Karim 2008.
35. Grewal 2013.
36. Karim 2008; Khabeer 2016.
37. Prickett 2015.
38. Rouse (2004) found African American Muslim women in her study doing the same.
39. Karim 2008.
40. Tavory 2016.
41. See Khabeer 2016.
42. Tavory 2016.
43. Wilde 2017.
44. Emerson 2006, 156.
45. Emerson 2006; see also Omi and Winant 1994.
46. Prickett 2015.
47. Emerson and Smith 2000, 161.

Conclusion

1. Ava and Avaline are both pseudonyms. I once told Ava and Aisha the names I had assigned them for this study. Ava hated hers. I asked whether she had another fake name she wanted me to use, and she replied, "Why can't *I* have a Muslim name, like Aisha?" I told her it would be disingenuous, since she didn't have a Muslim name in real life while Aisha did. Then Ava wanted me to use her real name, but I explained that I couldn't because of the restrictions of the Institutional Review Board application I had submitted before the start of the project. I couldn't think of any other name that would fit the real Ava, so I stuck with the one we had discussed. After her death, I savored the funny exchange as giving new meaning to the pseudonym.
2. One of Ava's daughters ordered the headstone, on which there is no mention of "Sister Ava" or anything about her being in a Muslim community. But it does include the two surnames, one of which is Muslim.
3. Tavory 2016.
4. Bagby 2012.
5. Bagby 2012, 5.
6. Pew Research 2017.
7. Besheer Mohammad, personal communication, 2017.
8. Abdullah 2010.
9. Durkheim 1965 [1912].
10. For more details on the story of Sister Sherri, please see Prickett (2019).

Appendix

1. For an example, see Watanabe and Esquivel 2009.
2. Eliasoph and Lichterman 2003.
3. Prickett 2015.
4. Avishai 2008; Mahmood 2005; O'Brien 2017; Rinaldo 2013; Rouse 2004; Tavory 2016.

5. Timmermans and Tavory 2012.
6. Tavory and Timmermans 2014.
7. Ganiel and Mitchell 2006.
8. Khabeer 2016.
9. Timmermans and Tavory 2012, 173.
10. Tavory and Timmermans 2014.
11. Parvez 2018.

References

Abdullah, Zain. 2010. *Black Mecca: The African Muslims of Harlem*. New York: Oxford University Press.

Abu-Lughod, Janet L. 2007. *Race, Space, and Riots in Chicago, New York, and Los Angeles*. New York: Oxford University Press.

Abu-Lughod, Lila. 2002. "Do Muslim Women Really Need Saving? Anthropological Reflections on Cultural Relativism and Its Others." *American Anthropologist* 104:783–90.

Abu-Lughod, Lila. 2013. *Do Muslim Women Need Saving?* Cambridge, MA: Harvard University Press.

Ammerman, Nancy 2014. "Finding Religion in Everyday Life." *Sociology of Religion* 75 (2): 189–207.

Anderson, Elijah. 1999. *Code of the Street: Decency, Violence, and the Moral Life of the Inner City*. New York: W. W. Norton.

Avishai, Orit. 2008. "'Doing Religion' in a Secular World: Women in Conservative Religions and the Question of Agency." *Gender and Society* 22 (4): 409–33.

Avishai, Orit. 2016. "Theorizing Gender from Religion Cases: Agency, Feminist Activism, and Masculinity." *Sociology of Religion* 77 (3): 261–79.

Bagby, Ihsan. 2012. *The American Mosque 2011: Basic Characteristics of the American Mosque*. Washington, DC: Council on American-Islamic Relations.

Bagby, Ihsan, Paul M. Pearl, and Bryan T. Froehle. 2001. *The Mosque in America: A National Portrait*. Washington, DC: Council on American-Islamic Relations.

Bail, Christopher. 2014. *Terrified: How Anti-Muslim Fringe Organizations Became Mainstream*. Princeton, NJ: Princeton University Press.

Baudrillard, Jean. 1981. *For a Critique of the Political Economy of the Sign*. St. Louis: Telos Press.

Bautista, Julius. 2008. "The Meta-theory of Piety: Reflections on the Work of Saba Mahmood." *Contemporary Islam* 2 (1): 75–83.

Bennett, Dionne. 2010. "Looking for the 'Hood and Finding Community: South Central, Race, and Media." In *Black Los Angeles: American Dreams and Racial Realities*, edited by D. Hunt and C. Ramon, 215–31. New York: New York University Press.

Beoku-Betts, Josephine. 1995. "We Got Our Way of Cooking Things: Women, Food, and Preservation of Cultural Identity among the Gullah." *Gender and Society* 9 (5): 535–55.

Beydoun, Khaled A. 2016. "Between Indigence, Islamophobia, and Erasure: Poor and Muslim in War on Terror America." *California Law Review* 104:1463.

Bilici, Mucahit. 2012. *Finding Mecca in America: How Islam Is Becoming an American Religion.* Chicago: University of Chicago Press.

Borden, Sam. 2012. "Observance of Ramadan Poses Challenges to Muslim Athletes." *New York Times,* August 1.

Buddi, Mahesh. 2018. "Hyderabad School Principal Gives Wife Triple Talaq over the Phone." *Times of India* (Hyderabad), December 21.

Butler, Judith. 2003. "Violence, Mourning, Politics." *Studies in Gender and Sexuality* 4 (1): 9–37.

Byng, Michelle D. 1998. "Mediating Discrimination: Resisting Oppression among African-American Muslim Women." *Social Problems* 45:473–87.

Calhoun-Brown, A. 1999. "The Image of God: Black Theology and Racial Empowerment in the African American Community." *Review of Religious Research* 40 (3): 197–212.

Chaddha, Anmol, and William Julius Wilson. 2011. "'Way Down in the Hole': Systemic Urban Inequality and the Wire." *Critical Inquiry* 38 (1): 164–88.

Chan-Malik, Sylvia. 2018. *Being Muslim: A Cultural History of Women of Color in American Islam.* New York: New York University Press.

Collins, Patricia Hill. 2000. *Black Feminist Thought: Knowledge, Consciousness, and the Politics of Empowerment.* 2nd ed. New York: Routledge.

Costa Vargas, João H. 2006. *Catching Hell in the City of Angels: Life and Meanings of Blackness in South Central Los Angeles.* Minneapolis: University of Minnesota Press.

Curtis, Edward E. 2002. *Islam in Black America: Identity, Liberation, and Difference in African-American Islamic Thought.* Albany: State University of New York Press.

Curtis, Edward E. 2006. *Black Muslim Religion in the Nation of Islam, 1960–1975.* Chapel Hill: University of North Carolina Press.

Davis, Mike. 1990. *City of Quartz: Excavating the Future in Los Angeles.* New York: Verso.

Dawson, Michael C. 2001. *Black Visions: The Roots of Contemporary African-American Political Ideologies.* Chicago: University of Chicago Press.

DeCaro, Louis A. 1996. *On the Side of My People: A Religious Life of Malcolm X.* New York: New York University Press.

Dow, Dawn Marie. 2015. "Negotiating 'the Welfare Queen' and 'the Strong Black Woman': African American Middle-Class Mothers' Work and Family Perspectives." *Sociological Perspectives* 58 (1): 36–55.

Durkheim, Emile. 1965 [1912]. *The Elementary Forms of Religious Life.* New York: Free Press.

Eliasoph, Nina, and Paul Lichterman. 2003. "Culture in Interaction." *American Journal of Sociology* 108 (4): 735–94.

Emerson, Michael O. 2006. *People of the Dream: Multiracial Congregations in the United States.* Princeton, NJ: Princeton University Press.

Emerson, Michael O., and Christian Smith. 2000. *Divided by Faith: Evangelical Religion and the Problem of Race in America.* New York: Oxford University Press.

Erikson, Kai T. 1978. *Everything in Its Path.* New York: Simon and Schuster.

Essien-Udom, E. U. 1962. *Black Nationalism: A Search for an Identity in America.* Chicago: University of Chicago Press.

Frederick, Marla. 2003. *Between Sundays: Black Women and Everyday Struggles of Faith.* Berkeley: University of California Press.

Flory, Richard, Brie Loskota, and Donald E. Miller. 2011. *Forging a New Moral and Political Agenda: The Civic Role of Religion in Los Angeles, 1992–2010.* Los Angeles: USC Center for Religion and Civic Culture.

Ganiel, Gladys, and Claire Mitchell. 2006. "Turning the Categories Inside-Out: Complex Identifications and Multiple Interactions in Religious Ethnography." *Sociology of Religion* 67 (1): 3–21.

Gans, Herbert. 2011. "The Moynihan Report and Its Aftermaths: A Critical Analysis." *Du Bois Review: Social Science Research on Race* 8 (2): 315–27.

Gardell, Mattias. 1996. *In the Name of Elijah Muhammad: Louis Farrakhan and the Nation of Islam.* Durham, NC: Duke University Press.

GhaneaBassiri, Kambiz. 2013. "Islamophobia and American History." In *Islamophobia in America*, pp. 53–74. New York: Palgrave Macmillan.

Gibson, Dawn-Marie, and Jamillah Karim. 2014. *Women of the Nation: Between Black Protest and Sunni Islam.* New York: New York University Press.

Goffman, Erving. 1952. "On Cooling the Mark Out: Some Aspects of Adaptation to Failure." *Psychiatry* 15 (4): 451–63.

Grant, David M., Melvin L. Oliver, and Angela D. James. 1996. "African Americans: Social and Economic Bifurcation." In *Ethnic Los Angeles*, edited by R. Waldinger and M. Bozorgmehr, 379–411. New York: Russell Sage Foundation.

Gregory, Steven. 1998. *Black Corona: Race and the Politics of Place in an Urban Community.* Princeton, NJ: Princeton University Press.

Grewal, Zareena. 2013. *Islam Is a Foreign Country: American Muslims and the Global Crisis of Authority.* New York: New York University Press.

Guhin, Jeffrey. 2018. "Colorblind Islam: The Racial Hinges of Immigrant Muslims in the United States." *Social Inclusion* 6 (2): 87–97.

Haddad, Yvonne Yazbeck, Jane I. Smith, and Kathleen M. Moore. 2006. *Muslim Women in America: The Challenge of Islamic Identity Today.* New York: Oxford University Press.

Hammack, Phillip L., David M. Frost, and Sam D. Hughes. 2019. "Queer Intimacies: A New Paradigm for the Study of Relationship Diversity." *Journal of Sex Research* 56 (4–5): 556–92.

Harris-Lacewell, Lacy. 2004. *Barbershops, Bibles, and BET: Everyday Talk and Black Political Thought.* Princeton, NJ: Princeton University Press.

Hochschild, Arlie. 2016. *Strangers in Their Own Land: Anger and Mourning on the American Right.* New York: New Press.

Hunt, Darnell. 1997. *Screening the Los Angeles "Riots": Race, Seeing, and Resistance.* New York: Cambridge University Press.

Hunt, Darnell. 2010. "Introduction: Dreaming of Black Los Angeles." In *Black Los Angeles: American Dreams and Racial Realities*, edited by D. Hunt and C. Ramon, 1–17. New York: New York University Press.

Hunter, Marcus Anthony. 2013. *Black Citymakers: How the Philadelphia Negro Changed Urban America.* New York: Oxford University Press.

Hunter, Marcus Anthony, Mary Pattillo, Zandria F. Robinson, and Keeanga-Yamahtta Taylor. 2016. "Black Placemaking: Celebration, Play, and Poetry." *Theory, Culture and Society* 33 (7–8): 31–56.

Hunter, Marcus Anthony, and Zandria F. Robinson. 2016. "The Sociology of Urban Black America." *Annual Review of Sociology* 42:385–405.

Inglehart, Ronald, and Pippa Norris. 2003. *Rising Tide: Gender Equality and Cultural Change around the World.* Cambridge: Cambridge University Press.

Jackson, Sherman. 2005. *Islam and the Blackamerican: Looking toward the Third Resurrection.* New York: Oxford University Press.

Kahera, Akel Ismail. 2002. *Deconstructing the American Mosque: Space, Gender, and Aesthetics.* Austin: University of Texas Press.

Karim, Jamillah. 2008. *American Muslim Women: Negotiating Race, Class, and Gender within the Ummah.* New York: New York University Press.

Kelley, Robin D. G. 1994. *Race Rebels: Culture, Politics, and the Black Working Class.* New York: Free Press.

Khabeer, Su'ad Abdul. 2016. *Muslim Cool: Race, Religion, and Hip Hop in the United States.* New York: New York University Press.

Kishi, Katayoun. 2017. "Assaults against Muslims in U.S. Surpass 2001 Level." Washington, DC: Pew Research Center. Retrieved at https://www.pewresearch.org/fact-tank/2017/11/15/assaults-against-muslims-in-u-s-surpass-2001-level/.

Kochuyt, Thierry. 2009. "God, Gifts and Poor People: On Charity in Islam." *Social Compass* 56 (1): 98–116.

Korteweg, Anna. 2008. "The Sharia Debate in Ontario: Gender, Islam, and Representations of Muslim Women's Agency." *Gender and Society* 22 (4): 434–54.

Kun, Josh, and Laura Pulido. 2013. *Black and Brown in Los Angeles: Beyond Conflict and Coalition.* Berkeley: University of California Press.

Laird, Lance D., and Wendy Cadge. 2009. "Constructing American Muslim Identity: Tales of Two Clinics in Southern California." *Muslim World* 99 (2): 270–93.

Lamont, Michele. 2000. *The Dignity of Working Men: Morality and the Boundaries of Race, Class, and Immigration.* Cambridge, MA: Harvard University Press.

Laslett, John H. M. 1996. "Historical Perspectives: Immigration and the Rise of a Distinctive Urban Region, 1900–1970." In *Ethnic Los Angeles*, edited by R. Waldinger and M. Bozorgmehr, 39–75. New York: Russell Sage Foundation.

Leonard, Karen Isaksen. 2003. *Muslims in the United States: The State of Research.* New York: Russell Sage Foundation.

Lincoln, C. Eric. 1994 [1961]. *The Black Muslims in America.* 3rd ed. Grand Rapids, MI: W. B. Eerdmans.

Love, Erik. 2017. *Islamophobia and Racism in America.* New York: New York University Press.

Macfarlane, Julie. 2012. *Islamic Divorce in North America: A Shari'a Path in a Secular Society.* New York: Oxford University Press.

Majeed, Debra. 2006. "Clara Evans Muhammad: Pioneering Social Activism in the Original Nation of Islam." In *The Encyclopedia of Women and Religion in North America*, edited by Rosemary S. Keller and Rosemary R. Ruether, 746–53. Bloomington: Indiana University Press.

Mahmood, Saba. 2001. "Feminist Theory, Embodiment, and the Docile Agent: Some Reflections on the Egyptian Islamic Revival." *Cultural Anthropology* 16 (2): 202–36.

Mahmood, Saba. 2005. *Politics of Piety: The Islamic Revival and the Feminist Subject.* Princeton. NJ: Princeton University Press.

Malcolm X. 1964. *The Autobiography of Malcolm X with the Assistance of Alex Haley.* New York: Castle Books.

Mamiya, Lawrence H. 1982. "From Black Muslim to Bilalian: The Evolution of a Movement." *Journal for the Scientific Study of Religion* 21 (2): 138–52.

Mauss, Marcel. 1954. *Gift: The Form and Reason for Exchange in Archaic Societies.* New York: W. W. Norton.

McRoberts, Omar. 2003. *Streets of Glory: Church and Community in a Black Urban Neighborhood.* Chicago: University of Chicago Press.

Mohamed, Besheer, and John O'Brien. 2011. "Ground Zero of Misunderstanding." *Contexts* 10 (1): 62–64.

Mol, Annemarie, Ingunn Moser, and Jeannette Pols, eds. 2010. *Care in Practice: On Tinkering in Clinics, Homes and Farms.* MatteRealities/VerKörperungen, vol. 8. Bielefeld, Germany: Transcript Verlag.

Nazish, Kiran. 2014. "For Muslims in New York, Observing Ramadan Is a Blend of Rituals Far and Near." *New York Times*, July 24.

Nelson, Timothy. 2005. *Every Time I Feel the Spirit: Religious Experience and Ritual in an African American Church*. New York: New York University Press.

Nembhard, Jessica Gordon. 2014. *Collective Courage: A History of African American Cooperative Economic Thought and Practice*. University Park: Penn State University Press.

O'Brien, John. 2017. *Keeping It Halal: The Everyday Lives of Muslim American Teenage Boys*. Princeton, NJ: Princeton University Press.

Omi, Michael, and Howard Winant. 1994. *Racial Formation in the United States: From the 1960s to the 1990s*. New York: Routledge.

Ong, Aihwa. 1995. "State versus Islam: Malay Families, Women's Bodies, and the Body Politic in Malaysia." In *Bewitching Women, Pious Men: Gender and Body Politics in Southeast Asia*, edited by Aihwa Ong and Michael G. Peletz, 159–94. Berkeley: University of California Press.

Ong, Paul, Alycia Cheng, Chhandara Pech, and Silvia R. Gonzalez. 2017. "1992 Revisited: Divergent Paths." Los Angeles: UCLA School of Public Affairs. Retrieved at http://www.aasc .ucla.edu/news/1992_Revisited_CNK.pdf.

Orsi, Robert A. 2003. "Is the Study of Lived Religion Irrelevant to the World We Live In?" *Journal for the Scientific Study of Religion* 42 (2): 169–74.

Parvez, Z. Fareen. 2018. "The Sorrow of Parting: Ethnographic Depth and the Role of Emotions." *Journal of Contemporary Ethnography* 47 (4): 454–83.

Pattillo, Mary. 1999. *Black Picket Fences: Privilege and Peril among the Black Middle Class*. Chicago: University of Chicago Press.

Pattillo, Mary. 2007. *Black on the Block: The Politics of Race and Class in the City*. Chicago: University of Chicago Press.

Pew Research Center. 2010. "Who Knows What about Religion." Washington, DC: Pew Research Center. https://www.pewforum.org/2010/09/28/u-s-religious-knowledge-survey -who-knows-what-about-religion/.

Pew Research Center. 2012. "The Global Religious Landscape." Washington, DC: Pew Research Center.

Pew Research Center. 2017. "How Americans Feel About Religious Groups." Washington, DC: Pew Research Center. https://www.pewforum.org/2017/02/15/americans-express-increas ingly-warm-feelings-toward-religious-groups/.

Pew Research Center. 2018. "Five Facts about the Religious Lives of African Americans." Washington, DC: Pew Research Center. https://www.pewresearch.org/fact-tank/2018/02 /07/5-facts-about-the-religious-lives-of-african-americans/.

Prickett, Pamela. 2014. "Contextualizing from Within: Perceptions of Physical Disorder in a South Central L.A. African American Mosque." *City and Community* 13 (3): 214–32.

Prickett, Pamela. 2015. "Negotiating Gendered Religious Space: The Particularities of Patriarchy in an African American Mosque." *Gender and Society* 29 (1): 51–72.

Prickett, Pamela. 2018. "Complexity beyond Intersections: Race, Class, and Neighborhood Disadvantage among African American Muslims." *Social Inclusion* 6 (2): 98–106.

Prickett, Pamela. 2019. "When the Road Is Covered in Nails: Making Sense of Madness in an Urban Mosque." *Social Problems*, https://doi.org/10.1093/socpro/spz057.

Putnam, Robert D. 2001. *Bowling Alone: The Collapse and Revival of American Community*. New York: Simon and Schuster.

Rehman, Javaid. 2007. "The Sharia, Islamic Family Laws and International Human Rights Law: Examining the Theory and Practice of Polygamy and Talaq." *International Journal of Law, Policy and the Family* 21 (1): 108–27.

Rinaldo, Rachel. 2013. *Mobilizing Piety: Islam and Feminism in Indonesia*. New York: Oxford University Press.

Rouse, Carolyn Moxley. 2004. *Engaged Surrender: African American Women and Islam.* Berkeley: University of California Press.

Roussell, Aaron. 2015. "Policing the Anticommunity: Race, Deterritorialization, and Labor Market Reorganization in South Los Angeles." *Law and Society Review* 49 (4): 813–45.

Scott, James C. 1985. *Weapons of the Weak: Everyday Forms of Peasant Resistance.* New Haven, CT: Yale University Press.

Sherman, Jennifer. 2009. *Those Who Work, Those Who Don't: Poverty, Morality, and Family in Rural America.* Minneapolis: University of Minnesota Press.

Siddiqi, Muzammil. 2014. "Chapter 9: Practicing Islam in the United States." In *The Oxford Handbook of American Islam,* edited by Yvonne Yazbeck Haddad and Jane I. Smith, 159–73. New York: Oxford University Press.

Sides, Josh. 2003. *L.A. City Limits: African American Los Angeles from the Great Depression to the Present.* Berkeley: University of California Press.

Sides, Josh. 2012. "Introduction: A Brief History of the American Ghetto." In *Post-Ghetto: Reimagining South Los Angeles,* edited by Josh Sides, 1–9. Berkeley and San Marino, CA: University of California Press and the Huntington Library.

Singer, Amy. 2008. *Charity in Islamic Societies.* New York: Cambridge University Press.

Small, Mario. 2008. "Four Reasons to Abandon the Idea of 'The Ghetto.'" *City and Community* 7 (4): 389–98.

Smith, Jane. 2010. *Islam in America.* 2nd ed. New York: Columbia University Press.

Stack, Carol. 1974. *All Our Kin: Strategies for Survival in a Black Community.* New York: Harper and Row.

Stiles, Erin E. 2003. "When Is a Divorce a Divorce? Determining Intention in Zanzibar's Islamic Courts." *Ethnology* 42 (4): 273–88.

St. Jean, Peter K. B. 2007. *Pockets of Crime: Broken Windows, Collective Efficacy, and the Criminal Point of View.* Chicago: University of Chicago Press.

Stuart, Forrest. 2016. *Down, Out, and Under Arrest: Policing and Everyday Life in Skid Row.* Chicago: University of Chicago Press.

Sullivan, Susan Crawford. 2012. *Living Faith: Everyday Religion and Mothers in Poverty.* Chicago: University of Chicago Press.

Tavory, Iddo. 2010. "Of Yarmulkes and Categories: Delegating Boundaries and the Phenomenology of Interactional Expectation." *Theory and Society* 39 (1): 49–68.

Tavory, Iddo. 2016. *Summoned: Identification and Religious Life in an Orthodox Jewish Neighborhood.* Chicago: University of Chicago Press.

Tavory, Iddo. 2018. "Between Situations: Anticipations, Rhythms and the Theory of Interaction." *Sociological Theory* 36 (2): 117–33.

Tavory, Iddo, and Stefan Timmermans. 2014. *Abductive Analysis: Theorizing Qualitative Research.* Chicago: University of Chicago Press.

Thieme, Tatiana. 2018. "The Hustle Economy: Informality, Uncertainty and the Geographies of Getting By." *Progress in Human Geography* 42 (4): 529–48.

Timmermans, Stefan, and Iddo Tavory. 2012. "Theory Construction in Qualitative Research: From Grounded Theory to Abductive Analysis." *Sociological Theory* 30 (3): 167–86.

Turner, Richard Brent. 1997. *Islam in the African American Experience.* Bloomington: Indiana University Press.

Vatuk, Sylvia. 2008. "Islamic Feminism in India: Indian Muslim Women Activists and the Reform of Muslim Personal Law." *Modern Asian Studies* 42 (2–3): 489–518.

Venkatesh, Sudhir A. 1997. "The Social Organization of Street Gang Activity in an Urban Ghetto." *American Journal of Sociology* 103 (1): 82–111.

Venkatesh, Sudhir A. 2006. *Off the Books: The Underground Economy of the Urban Poor*. Cambridge, MA: Harvard University Press.

Wacquant, Loïc. 2008. *Urban Outcasts: A Comparative Sociology of Advanced Marginality*. Malden, MA: Polity.

Wadud, Amina. 2006. *Inside the Gender Jihad: Women's Reform in Islam*. London: Oneworld Publications.

Watanabe, Teresa, and Paloma Esquivel. 2009. "L.A. Area Muslims Say FBI Surveillance Has a Chilling Effect on Their Free Speech and Religious Practices." *Los Angeles Times*, March 1.

Wilde, Melissa. 2017. "Complex Religion: Interrogating Assumptions of Independence in the Study of Religion." *Sociology of Religion* 79 (3): 287–98.

Wilde, Melissa J., and Patricia Tevington. 2017. "Complex Religion: Toward a Better Understanding of the Ways in Which Religion Intersects with Inequality." In *Emerging Trends in the Social Sciences*, edited by Robert Scott and Marlis Buchmann with Stephen Kosslyn, 1–13. Hoboken, NJ: John Wiley and Sons, https://doi.org/10.1002/9781118900772.etr ds0440.

Williams, Rhys. 2011. "Creating an American Islam: Thoughts on Religion, Identity, and Place." *Sociology of Religion* 72 (2): 127–53.

Wilson, William Julius. 1987. *The Truly Disadvantaged: The Inner City, the Underclass, and Public Policy*. Chicago: University of Chicago Press.

Wilson, William Julius. 1996. *When Work Disappears: The World of the New Urban Poor*. New York: Vintage Books.

Winchester, Daniel. 2008. "Embodying the Faith: Religious Practice and the Making of a Muslim Moral Habitus." *Social Forces* 86 (4): 1753–80.

Wolfe, Alan. 2003. *The Transformation of American Religion: How We Actually Live Our Faith*. Chicago: University of Chicago Press.

Zelizer, Viviana. 2010. *Economic Lives: How Culture Shapes the Economy*. Princeton, NJ: Princeton University Press.

Zerubavel, Eviatar. 1989. *The Seven Day Circle: The History and Meaning of the Week*. Chicago: University of Chicago Press.

Zerubavel, Eviatar. 2003. *Time Maps: Collective Memory and the Social Shape of the Past*. Chicago: University of Chicago Press.

Index

Aisha, Sister, 9, 15, 23, 33, 60, 62–63, 74, 78–79, 91, 98, 109, 143–44

al-Islam, 10, 89–91, 100, 129, 150n35. *See also* African American Islam; Sunni Islam

American dream, 33, 47

American Islam, 104; class and racial differences within, 105; racialized boundaries, between African American and immigrant, 105–6

anti-Blackness, 107–8

Arab Americans, 107–8, 115–16, 122, 139

Asia, 43, 104, 136

Atlanta (Georgia), 156n25

Ava, Sister, 1, 6, 8–9, 15, 35, 42, 62, 76, 78–80, 83, 90–93, 97, 103, 111, 115, 126, 132, 133, 151n32, 157n2; burial service of, 127; death of, 124, 143

belonging, 10, 52, 96, 100

Black Americans. *See* African Americans

Black Business Bazaar, 54

Blackness, 47, 106, 108, 116, 128

Black placemaking, 10, 100; living Islam, 129

Boston (Massachusetts), 23; Four Corners, 24

boundary crossing, 122

boundary making, 36

Bradley, Tom, 52

Burhan, Sheikh, 108–13, 142

Butler, Judith, 135, 143

Catholicism, 6

Central America, 6, 55, 117

Chan-Malik, Sylvia, 89–91

charity, 119, 128, 150n5; feelings of difference, with outsiders, 120–21; moral superiority, perceptions of, 121; and piety, 121; race, as primary identity marker, 121

Chicago (Illinois), 41, 43–46, 51–52, 56, 156n25

Christianity, 7, 107

civic religion, 36

Civil Rights movement, 113

class, 13, 89, 101, 115, 119–20, 122–23, 127, 130, 140–41; race, intersection of, 105

Collins, Patricia Hill, 90, 155n24

Combahee River Collective, 155n24

communality, 22–23

community building, 20

complementarity, 89

cult of domesticity, 155n31; and piety, 89

culture, as kind of theatre, 70

deep story, 83

democracy, 36

Detroit (Michigan), 43–45

din (faith), 3, 95, 119, 128–29; good intentions, 27; sisterhood networks, 96

"do for self" ideology, 70; care work, as form of, 69; and entrepreneurialism, 82–83

Dow, Dawn Marie, 89

drug trade, 38, 56–57

Egypt, 3, 19, 27

Eid al-Fitr holiday, 64, 80, 104, 118, 150n8; charitable giving, 119

embodied practices, 27, 37

endurance, 26, 100

entrepreneurialism, 82–83

Erikson, Kai, 70

Essien-Udom, E. U., 152n7

ethnic boundary making, 107

ethnography, 143–44

Excellence in Learning Charter School (EIL), 59, 116–18

Fard, W. D., 43–45, 53, 61, 86–87, 152n7

Fareed, Brother, Sr., 30–31, 41–42, 57, 60–62, 73, 98, 130–31, 141, 143, 151n32

Farrakhan, Louis, 13

fasting, 4, 15–16, 18–19, 21–22, 25, 30, 34, 103

Federal Bureau of Investigation (FBI), 105; COINTELPRO operations, 152n36

fellowshipping, 6, 122

feminism, 88, 101; sexes, equality between, 89

frame switching: boundary flexing, allowing of, 25; moral cartography, 25

Frye, Marquette, 51

gangs, 24–25, 30, 151n32; in prison, 109–10

Garveyite Black Cross Nurses, 46

gender, 13, 33, 127, 130; American authorities on Islam, 115–16; gendered bound-

Tocqueville, Alexis de, 36
Truth, Sojourner, 86
Tubman, Harriet, 86

ummah (community of all believers), 106,
110, 113, 116, 121–23, 128; class and race,
intersection of, 105; diversity of, 104–5,
136; economic differences, 105; stratification within, 105
United States, 4–5, 9, 14, 47–48, 59, 68,
77, 90–92, 101, 112, 114–16, 140, 156n25;
ethnic boundary making in, 107; Islam
in, 129–30; mosques in, 12, 107, 110, 129;
Muslim population in, 104–5, 127; "new
races" in, 113; race in, 107; religious congregations in, 122; riots in, 51; white racial
dominance, legacy of, 106
University of California at Los Angeles

(UCLA), Institutional Review Board
(IRB), 73, 139, 157n11
University of Islam schools, 47, 53. *See also*
Sister Clara Muhammad schools

Venkatesh, Sudhir, 28

Wacquant, Loïc, 112
Watts, 51, 152n29
white supremacy, 106, 108
Wilde, Melissa, 149n11
womanist theology, 155n24; collective religious ethos of, 89
women's mosque movement, 3, 27
World Trade Center, 122
World War II, 49

zakat (charity), 16, 26, 36, 119, 128–29, 150n5